WRITE WITH POWER AND CONFIDENCE

Writing Techniques and Book-Industry Practices Every Author Should Know

WRITE WITH POWER AND CONFIDENCE

Writing Techniques and Book-Industry Practices Every Author Should Know

DUANE S. CROWTHER

Second Printing: March, 2004

International Standard Book Number:
0-88290-621-6

Horizon Publishers' Catalog and Order Number:
1212

Printed and distributed
in the United States of America by

Horizon Publishers

& Distributors, Incorporated

Mailing Address:
P.O. Box 490
Bountiful, Utah 84011-0490

Street Address:
50 South 500 West
Bountiful, Utah 84010

Local Phone: (801) 295-9451
Toll Free: 1 (866) 818-6277
FAX: (801) 295-0196

E-mail: horizonp@burgoyne.com

Website: http://wwww.horizonpublishersbooks.com

Dedication

This book is lovingly dedicated to my wife, *Jean*, for all her great love, support, inspiration, and wisdom. She brings continual joy to my life!

It also is dedicated to my children and their mates, who maintain our family ties, and whose loving concern and innate goodness are a source of ongoing happiness to me:

Don and Cheryl,
Scott and Liz,
Lisa and Mike,
David and Kris,
Bill and Becky,
Sharon and Chet,
Laura, and
Bethany

And it is dedicated with love to all my grandchildren, who bring sweetness and laughter into my life, and who entertain and impress me as I watch their growth. I stand in awe of who they are and what they are becoming:

Megan, Marsali and *Jacob,*
Christina, Sarah, Matt, Jon, and *Timothy,*
Carson, Caroline, Adam and *Jesse Decker,*
Joshua, Jenna, and *Kellie,*
Landon and *Calvin,*
Kendra,
and those who are still to come

Acknowledgments

It takes a good support team to produce a book such as ***Write With Power and Confidence***. With any book, the author typically has the idea, the inspiration, the creative urge, and the plan upon which the book is constructed, but it is equally true that there are others who help in that book's design and production. So it was with the creation of this book.

My help came from the production staff at Horizon Publishers. Sam Richardson, our typesetter, carried a major portion of the load. With all the charts and varied layouts, this certainly was not an easy book to commit to Quark Express. He did an admirable job!

Karyl Dowling, our pre-press manager, moved the book down the production schedule, aiding in many ways and moving the book to completion, first on the MicroPress, and then on the full press and bindery assembly line. It was she who produced the first advertising mail pieces and got them into print on a tight deadline.

Jean Crowther and Larry Brady, who both have editorial responsibilities at Horizon Publishers, gave assistance with typing the best-seller lists, indexing, proofreading, and generally moving the book toward completion. Jean did most of the indexing and typed the rough drafts of several chapters. Larry created the Excel database templates for the Fiction Writing and Non-Fiction Writing Manuscript Scorecards.

The cover design committee at Horizon Publishers, consisting of the author plus Richard Hopkins, Karyl Dowling, Larry Brady and Sam Richardson, engaged in their usual lively debate about the cover and its contents. There's always a diversity of opinions as to what is good design, and it takes a while to reach consensus.

Thanks are extended, also, to the entire staff of Horizon Publishers for their efforts in printing and binding the book, processing advertising, participating in sales activities, telemarketing, handling the invoicing and shipping, and doing all those tasks which make the introduction of a new book to the marketplace a successful venture. Everyone contributes their best efforts, and those efforts are truly appreciated!

Contents

1

Guidelines for Writing Great Fiction

INTRODUCTION

Books galore have been written that teach the basic skills of crafting fiction. This chapter is an extensive summary of many of those teachings. ***Three hundred and forty-nine key points*** have been assembled, reduced to one-line phrases, and then organized into twenty-two overall headings. These headings are grouped into three main divisions: ***story***, ***structure***, and ***style***.

To help you evaluate your work, all these principles are presented in this chapter in a Fiction Manuscript Scorecard. This scorecard is a tool the author devised for use in his publishing company. Other publishers have adapted it to their needs and are using it also. But while it helps publishers select manuscripts for publication, its greatest value is as an evaluation tool which authors can use to judge the quality of their own work. That's why it is made available in this context. Authors who carefully critique their own work, identifying areas of strength upon which they capitalize, and also determining areas of weakness which they conscientiously strive to correct, save themselves from the inconvenience of many hours lost and the pain of many rejection notices received.

The concepts summarized here are truly valuable pearls. Sometimes they will open up new vistas of creative thought. Sometimes they will trigger responses which solve serious problems in your writing. No matter how you use them, many such conceptual pearls are here for you. Study them carefully and learn from them.

Be sure to actually use them as evaluation tools. Use each tool to guide your analysis as you carefully evaluate every aspect of your manuscript. Grade yourself from one to ten on each of the twenty-two overall criteria, and on each of the many sub-concepts found in those criteria. Be brutally frank in your evaluation—that's what will help you to grow. Obviously, not all of the listed concepts will be directly applicable to your writing. Choose the ideas that apply to what you've written and save the conflicting ideas for the manuscript you'll write next year. After you've gone through the entire process, go back and select the areas where you scored yourself the lowest, and use the concepts to guide your rewriting efforts.

Fiction Manuscript Scorecard

Title ______________________________________

Author ______________________ Ms. # __________

Evaluated by______________________ Date __________

Criteria	Weight	Score	Weighted Score	Average
Story				
1. Plot and Story Idea	3	____	____	
2. Story Flow and Pace	2	____	____	
3. Conflict	2	____	____	
4. Suspense	2	____	____	
5. Characterization	3	____	____	
6. Protagonist (Hero)	2	____	____	
7. Antagonist (Villain)	2	____	____	
8. Dialogue	3			
				____
Structure				
9. Main Title, Chapter Titles	2	____	____	
10. Beginning	2	____	____	
11. Middle	1	____	____	
12. Climax	2	____	____	
13. Ending	1	____	____	
14. Chapter and Scene Structure	1	____	____	
15. Settings and Atmosphere	1			
				____
Style				
16. Author Intrusions	1	____	____	
17. Style	2	____	____	
18. Writing Technique	3	____	____	
19. Use of Basic Writing Principles	3	____	____	
20. Word Preferences	1	____	____	
21. Grammatical Usage	2	____	____	
22. Polishing and Rewriting	3			
				____
Total Scores				

Scoring Key:

1=Very low
2=Low
3=Well below average
4=Below average
5=Low average
6=High average
7=Well above average
8=Excellent
9=Superior
10=Truly exceptional

HOW TO USE THE FICTION-WRITING MANUSCRIPT SCORECARD

1. ***Make photo copies of the form provided*** on page 16. This will allow repeated use of the form. Be sure a blank copy is kept on file as a photo-copy master.
2. ***Evaluate the manuscript under consideration, assigning a score for each criterion.*** Grade each of the twenty-two factors on a score range of 1-10. The following grade scale may be used or adapted:

1 = Very low	6 = High average
2 = Low	7 = Well above average
3 = Well below average	8 = Excellent
4 = Below average	9 = Superior
5 = Low average	10 = Truly exceptional

   Write the score for each category in the *Score* column to the left of the weighted scores. Use the above evaluation criteria explanations as guidelines.
3. ***Determine the weighted score for each category.*** Weight represents the relative importance the publisher or author assigns to each criterion. Multiply the *weight* times the *score* for each category, writing the result in the *Weighted Score* column.
4. ***Total the Weighted Score column.*** This will give a numerical evaluation for the manuscript which can be compared against other manuscript evaluations to aid in selecting the best manuscripts available or to indicate the strengths and weaknesses of the manuscript being evaluated. Finalize your analysis so it will be similar to the example on page 19.
5. ***Customize the scorecard if desired.*** The importance of each criterion may be perceived differently by various publishing companies or individual authors. The scorecard can be easily customized by changing the relative weights of the various criteria.

6. ***Set up a scorecard program on computer for easy evaluation.*** Reproduce the scorecard on a spreadsheet program so that evaluation results can be easily entered and printed out. If several evaluations are obtained for each manuscript, additional columns can be added to the right, and the individual evaluations can be programmed to add together into a grand total.

Greater value will be added if you take each of the criteria on pages 20 through 33 and put them into a spreadsheet program so you can evaluate each separate item individually. It is evaluation at that level that will help you discover the corrections you should make that will significantly raise the quality of your manuscript.

Fiction Scorecard Example

Title ______________________________

Author ____________________ Ms. # __________

Evaluated by ____________________ Date __________

Criteria	Weight	Score	Weighted Score	Average
Story				
1. Plot and Story Idea	3	7	21	
2. Story Flow and Pace	2	6	12	
3. Conflict	2	8	16	
4. Suspense	2	9	18	
5. Characterization	3	5	15	
6. Protagonist (Hero)	2	3	6	
7. Antagonist (Villain)	2	8	16	
8. Dialogue	3	4	12	
		50	116	6.1
Structure				
9. Main Title, Chapter Titles	2	8	16	
10. Beginning	2	7	14	
11. Middle	1	8	8	
12. Climax	2	6	12	
13. Ending	1	9	9	
14. Chapter and Scene Structure	1	5	5	
15. Settings and Atmosphere	1	6	6	
		49	70	7.0
Style				
16. Author Intrusions	1	8	8	
17. Style	2	6	12	
18. Writing Technique	3	7	21	
19. Use of Basic Writing Principles	3	5	15	
20. Word Preferences	1	7	7	
21. Grammatical Usage	2	4	8	
22. Polishing and Rewriting	3	9	27	
		46	98	6.5
Total Scores		145	284	6.5

Scoring Key:

		7=Well above average
1=Very low	4=Below average	8=Excellent
2=Low	5=Low average	9=Superior
3=Well below average	6=High average	10=Truly exceptional

FICTION EVALUATION CRITERIA

1. Plot and Story Idea

- is fresh, original, interesting, unique, intriguing, arouses curiosity
- is believable, realistic, true to life
- has a unifying theme
- is built upon a problem or situation of universal significance, not just local interest
- follows a coherent plan of development and resolution, achieving the desired end through cause-and-effect action
- contains elements of truth, timelessness, universality
- is not too complex or involved
- is not predictable nor contrived
- fulfills the primary function of fiction: *to entertain the reader*
- creates an emotion within the reader:

• suspense	• hope	• comfort
• sympathy	• determination	• inspiration
• amusement	• courage	• love

- involves the reader so he/she lives the story along with the characters

2. Story Flow and Pace

- moves fast and continually, is uninterrupted
- uses short words and sentences to speed the story's pace
- the reader's curiosity remains whetted
- the reader is kept in a state of near-perpetual surprise
- there is always an unsolved mystery or unresolved problem
- dramatic incidents move and build the story and maintain suspense
- clues are planted in the right places to lead to the ending

3. Conflict

- ***four basic situations:*** conflicts between
  - man and man
  - man and nature
  - man and self
  - man and God

- ***three powerful urges:***
  - life drive for self-preservation
  - love (includes loyalty and pity)
  - power—a desire to dominate and use an office for selfish ends
- ***three problem types:***
  - ***purpose problem:*** the hero is willing to fight to accomplish a goal or purpose
  - ***situation problem:*** the hero is trying to change an existing or just-occurred situation
  - ***decision problem:*** the hero must decide what to do in a tug-of-war with pulls of equal strength
- ***five basic needs:***
  - to love and be loved
  - to belong
  - to achieve
  - to have security (material, emotional, spiritual)
  - to know
- the problem is vital to the main character(s)
- the characters' struggle to solve the problem(s) is shown
- the obstacles are believable
- the characters react emotionally to other characters in a way consistent with their makeup
- the conflict emphasizes an emotion or a character trait
- the characters solve the problem; the resolution doesn't just happen
- the conflict is of interest to the targeted reader
- the consequences of failure are serious
- the reader knows the characters' motives and driving forces so he/she can recognize the significance of the characters' actions
- the conflict rouses curiosity or anxiety
- odds increase against the hero so that achieving the goal appears increasingly unattainable

4. Suspense

- keeps the reader interested in what will happen next
- makes the reader want to read on to answer questions
- the tone provokes a sense of mystery
- arises from the balanced struggle between the protagonist and the circumstances he must overcome
- there are enough plot furtherances and hindrances to lend suspense
- the outcome is always in doubt until the end
- the suspense is created by characters plus anxiety
- conflict and suspense are used in balanced proportions

5. Characterization

- clearly defined, real people
- believable characters are credibly motivated with realistic motives and antagonisms
- shows their human qualities, abilities, ambitions, temperaments, traits, characters, reactions
- depicts what they say, do, think
- the characters are appealing, memorable
- the characters are reasonable in their motivations
- the characters are willing to fight for their goals without self-pity
- minor characters are not so interesting they steal the story
- the characters are re-portrayed and re-identified as the story progresses

6. Protagonist (Hero)

- is someone with whom the reader can empathize
- has an important problem or goal
- has some specific desire, and feels threatened in his pursuit of that desire
- wants possession, relief or revenge
- is memorable
- is introduced very early in the story
- is a doer, not a "people watcher"
- major traits of the protagonist are repeatedly stressed
- the major character experiences character growth

7. Antagonist (Villain)

- competes with the hero's strength, skill and cleverness
- is almost equally matched with the hero
- his character flaws are contrasted with the hero's virtues
- is not wholly evil, but his negative qualities outweigh his positive ones
- is interesting, but not so fascinating he steals the reader's cheers from the hero
- must eventually be foiled; the hero must win
- has an unusual name which suits his character
- a powerful villain is needed to sustain dramatic, suspenseful plot action

8. Dialogue

- informs the reader
- characterizes the speaker
- shows the speaker's viewpoint
- moves the action, speeds up the story
- intensifies emotion
- adds local color and atmosphere
- listeners' reactions are indicated with actions, not with awkward adverbs used to label emotions
- no character is allowed to monopolize the conversation
- long speeches are broken up with action
- the speaker is clearly identified or indicated
- speaker identification is subtle, unobtrusive
- the dialogue is so representative of the participating characters that it unfolds without the author continually having to identify the speakers
- speeches are selective, never allowed to ramble, always advance the plot
- speeches are not stilted nor artificial (contractions are appropriate in dialogue)
- uses "said" rarely and effectively, utilizes good substitute words when appropriate
- characters don't all sound the same
- the speaker's tone of voice, choice of words, speaking tempo, facial expressions, gestures and mannerisms are portrayed

9. Main Title, Chapter Titles

Main Title

- is easily pronounced
- is easily understood
- is brief (usually 5 words or less, preferably 2 or 3 words)
- is original
- catches the reader's interest, arrests his attention (jumps off the page)
- is specific, appropriate, not misleading
- is fresh and alive, with color and excitement; not lifeless or limp

Chapter Titles

- are specific, appropriate, not misleading
- are fresh and alive, have color and excitement
- give clues to the story but don't reveal the story's outcomes
- promise what the book will deliver
- are slanted towards the reader and the market
- rely on active verbs, concrete "picture" nouns

10. Beginning

- "hooks" the reader and claims immediate attention
- begins at a high point of interest and action
- the protagonist is introduced early
- the protagonist's central problem is defined early and grabs the reader
- is intense
- has impact
- doesn't introduce too much background in the first sentences and paragraphs
- introduces the characters
- sets the stage
- sets the mood
- extends to the point where the problem confronting the protagonist is clearly defined

11. Middle

- clarifies the main character's motivation and reveals how he/she copes with the situation
- presents a course of ups and downs, furtherances and hindrances
- begins to fulfill the interesting promises presented in the beginning
- chapters end at crucial suspenseful moments to sustain interest
- scenes expand the story outline into dramatized units of action
- scenes grow logically out of previous scenes
- each scene has a new conflict, struggle, or solving of a problem
- scenes are a series of progressive events related to the central story idea
- scenes move the story forward
- scenes develop logically as they move toward the climax
- scenes prepare and develop the characters for the climax
- real obstacles keep the protagonist from achieving his major goal too easily
- scenes clearly show the problem intensifying

12. Climax

- is clearly the high point of the action
- usually involves an action or decision by the protagonist which leads to the resolution of the problem
- comes at a "black" moment when seemingly all is lost for the hero
- the protagonist is the character most affected by the climax
- climax tasks are done dramatically, succinctly, and with strong emotional impact
- represents the moment of decision, the point of no return
- intensity, emotion and interest reach their highest point
- the climax is immediately followed by the resolution of the problem
- is satisfying, logical, and rewards the reader

- surprise twists which deceive or cheat the reader are avoided
- solutions stem from the characters, not from coincidence nor outside sources
- is logical, credible

13. Ending

- solves the problem with firm finality
- reveals the main characters' thoughts and feelings
- has emotional impact and "punch"
- is not anticlimactic
- ties up loose ends
- pleases, rewards, satisfies, and doesn't cheat the reader
- shows how, when, why
- resolves conflicts, draws conclusions, makes projections
- makes the story memorable
- a "clincher" or "twist" at the end clearly answers the reader's question: "so what?"
- stops when the story is over

14. Chapter and Scene Structure

- each chapter is self-contained
- each chapter starts someplace, leads someplace, ends someplace
- transitions: movements from one scene to another are clearly defined
- situations further the plot and keep it moving
- situations develop characters through roadblocks which help or hinder them
- incidents go somewhere, contribute to the story, make a point

15. Settings and Atmosphere

- the atmosphere is expressed by the characters' actions and emotions
- the background information doesn't interrupt the story flow
- the background technical data is accurate and the background is realistic

- the scene settings convey a specific environment and emotional atmosphere
- the senses are used to suggest settings and images
- descriptions are short, colorful, and broken up by action and dialogue
- the story's mood is its "key": major, minor, high, low
- the story's mood colors the characters' thinking and responses

16. Author Intrusions

General Items:

- the author doesn't intrude into the story
- the author doesn't preach or moralize
- the author doesn't get ahead of the story
- the author lets characters speak for themselves
- the author lets the reader discover the theme from the characters' words
- the author refrains from injecting personal opinions
- the author doesn't break into the story with questions addressed to the reader

Transitions:

- connect words, ideas, and scenes smoothly
- move characters from place to place, time to time, or emotion to emotion
- serve as a shortcut, moving from "here" to "there" fast
- scenes are linked together with carry-over features
- transition words are clearly positioned at the beginning of sentences which contain little detail so they're easily recognized

Attention to Details:

- no details are left unresolved
- no characters are unaccounted for

Emphasis:

- avoids overuse of exclamation points, italics, bold, underlined words, words in all capital letters

Overworked Words:

- avoids the use of amateur and overworked words:
    - very
    - have
    - had
    - so
    - seems
    - then
    - but
    - just
    - oh
- avoids the use of overworked adverbs
    - almost
    - actually
    - practically
    - naturally
    - virtually
    - suddenly
    - really
    - absolutely
    - probably
    - obviously
    - undoubtedly
    - definitely
    - positively
- avoids the use of trite phrasing
    - it goes without saying
    - as you must know
    - as you can see
    - there is reason to believe that
- is not redundant—needless extra words which restate what's already said have been eliminated
- is free from clichés
- is free from anachronisms (people, places, things and words used out of their proper time or setting)

17. Style

- is indicated by the author's selection and arrangement of words—his/her vocabulary, flow of words, colorful phrases, and general tone
- may be
    - scholarly
    - dignified
    - flowery
    - anecdotal
    - humorous
    - breezy
    - homey
    - cynical
    - carefree
    - formal
    - arduous
    - preachy
    - light and funny
    - heavy and dull
    - conversational
    - picturesque
    - textbookish
    - philosophical
- reveals the author's personality—life outlook, education, beliefs, ethics, and imagination
- is shown in his originality, discipline, ability to arouse emotions, and technical mastery of the writer's craft
- has reserved ease, is not self-conscious
- is not imitative of others
- has a ready vocabulary

18. Writing Technique

Modern Style:

- uses terse, efficient prose
- the writing is tight, carefully constructed, to the point
- avoids outdated techniques (long descriptive passages, rambling wordiness)
- uses up-to-date language, story themes, and story outcomes
- avoids outdated slang, expressions and clichés

Sentence Usage:

- sentences vary in length and type
- make good sense, are clearly understood and not confusing
- are not choppy, cluttered, nor rambling
- are not long and complicated
- have the most important word near the beginning or end
- run-on sentences are avoided

Paragraph Usage:

- sentences follow in logical sequence
- paragraphs vary in length and sentence type
- most are less than 125 words in length
- paragraphs have a topic sentence which expresses the central thought

Narrative:

- is kept to a minimum; most of the story is told through dialogue and description
- the author shows the story through his/her characters rather than tells it
- the narrator is a participant, not a bystander

Point of View:

- remains constant throughout the story
- remains either first or third person
- if multiple points of view are used, the author makes as few shifts as possible
- avoids a "they" viewpoint
- avoids an omniscient all-knowing multiple viewpoint

Objective or Subjective Writing:

- objective writing tells what the character does
- subjective writing tells what the character thinks
- does not continually shift between the two writing approaches in the story

Flashbacks:

- provide needed background information
- clarify or intensify present action
- explain why characters act the way they do
- don't interrupt current action nor spoil the story's continuity
- are used with restraint, are not overused
- are brief and concise
- are entered and exited with good transitions
- don't raise questions concerning the main story's chronology

19. Use of Basic Writing Principles

Clarity:

- ideas are clear
- all parts of the idea are expressed
- ideas cannot be misunderstood

Unity:

- all parts are related
- all parts contribute to one clear overall idea
- the theme, point of view, mood and tense are constant, consistent and unchanging

Coherence:

- all parts are arranged in logical order
- all relationships are clearly expressed

Conciseness:

- ideas are expressed with brevity and economy

Emphasis:

- important ideas are arranged to show their importance
- key words are usually near the beginning or end of sentences

- key ideas are usually at the beginning or end of paragraphs

Interest:

- ideas are expressed effectively so they attract and hold reader interest
- ideas are of sufficient quality that they merit reader interest

20. Word Preferences

- prefers familiar words, not unfamiliar ones
- prefers Saxon words, not Romance words (uses English or German rather than French, Italian, Spanish, Portuguese, etc.)
- prefers nouns and verbs, not adjectives and adverbs
- prefers short words, not long ones
- prefers concrete words, not general ones
- prefers single words, not phrases
- prefers simple sentences, not complex ones
- prefers active voice, not passive voice
- prefers picture nouns, not non-image nouns
- prefers action verbs, not forms of the verb "to be"
- prefers action verbs, not adverb-verb combinations
- prefers action verbs, not inactive verbs
- prefers short paragraphs, not long paragraphs
- prefers original words and phrases, not trite ones
- prefers past tense, not past perfect tense
- prefers the specific, not the general
- prefers the concrete, not the abstract

21. Language Usage

- uses correct grammar
- uses correct punctuation
- uses correct spelling
- uses correct structure, form and technique
- uses lively and varied vocabulary
- uses words that create moods through their rhythm and inner sound and through the images they invoke

- uses words that make interesting and pleasing sounds (***assonance:*** resemblance of sounds in words and syllables, especially vowels; repetition of vowels without repetition of consonants (as in *holy* and *story*); used as an alternative to rhyme in verse; ***alliteration:*** the repetition of initial consonant sounds in two or more neighboring words or syllables (as *thr*eatening *thr*ongs, *wi*ld and *wo*oly); ***onomatopoeia:*** the naming of a thing or action by a vocal imitation of the sound associated with it (as *buzz, hiss*); the use of words whose sound suggests the sense of the statement
- uses show-and-tell words that paint pictures through the imagery of metaphors and similes
- avoids flowery, sentimental, preachy, and unnecessary words

22. Polishing and Rewriting

- the complete absence of careless errors gives clear evidence of extensive polishing and thorough proofreading
- superfluous words have been deleted
- involved sentences have been simplified
- the manuscript has professional tone, sparkle and style
- careless errors have been eliminated
- computer printouts are double-spaced, flush left, unjustified right
- grammar has been corrected; computer grammar-check programs have been used (but not to excess)
- spelling has been corrected; computer spell-checks have been made
- punctuation has been corrected
- word accuracy has been corrected
    - contains no incorrect words which escaped spell-checks
    - has no omitted words
- computer keyboarding has been corrected so the book can be typeset from the author's disk:
    - no hard returns in the middle of paragraphs
    - no inappropriate hard hyphens
    - indents are from tabs, not manually spaced over

- no imbedded hidden commands are on the disk (computer indexing, computer table of contents, etc.)
- basic, readable fonts are used (no script or ornate fonts)
- extensive use of bold, italic and underlining is avoided
- footnotes, endnotes and bibliographies are uniform in style and follow formats recommended in acceptable style manuals
- footnotes/endnotes begin at 1 with each new chapter

2

Guidelines for Writing Great Non-Fiction

INTRODUCTION

There are dozens of books that teach basic writing skills. This chapter is an extensive summary of many of those teachings. Unlike chapter one, which deals with writing fiction, this chapter is pointed towards expository writing. ***Three hundred and thirty-one key points*** have been assembled, reduced to one-line phrases, and then organized into twenty-five overall headings. These headings are grouped into three main divisions: ***subject and audience***, ***content and structure***, and ***style and technique***.

To help you evaluate your work, all these principles are presented in this chapter in an Expository-Writing Manuscript Scorecard. This scorecard is a tool the author devised for use in his publishing company. Other publishers have adapted it to their needs and are using it also. But while it helps publishers select manuscripts for publication, its greatest value is as an evaluation tool which authors can use to judge the quality of their own work. That's why it is made available in this context. Authors who carefully critique their own work, identifying areas of strength upon which they capitalize, and also determining areas of weakness which they conscientiously strive to correct, save themselves from the inconvenience of many hours lost and the pain of many rejection notices received.

The concepts summarized here are truly valuable writing tools. Sometimes they will open up new vistas of creative thought. Sometimes they will trigger responses which solve serious problems in your writing. No matter how you use them, many such conceptual tools are here for you. Study them carefully and learn from them.

Be sure to actually use them as evaluation tools. Use each tool to guide your analysis as you carefully evaluate every aspect of your manuscript. Grade yourself from one to ten on each of the twenty-five overall criteria, and on each of the many sub-concepts found in those criteria. Be brutally frank in your evaluation—that's what will help you to grow. Obviously, not all of the listed concepts will be directly applicable to your writing. Choose the ideas that apply to what you've written and save the conflicting ideas for the manuscript you'll write next year. After you've gone through the entire process, go back and select the areas where you scored yourself the lowest, and use the concepts to guide your rewriting efforts.

Expository-Writing Manuscript Scorecard

Title ______________________________

Author ____________________ Ms. # __________

Evaluated by ____________________ Date __________

Criteria	Weight	Score	Weighted Score	Average
Subject & Audience				
1. Significance of Subject	____	____	____	
2. Motivational Impact	____	____	____	
3. Reader Demand	____	____	____	
4. Reader Benefits	____	____	____	
5. Audience Definition	____	____	____	
6. Author's Credentials	____	____	____	
				____
Content & Structure				
7. Research	____	____	____	
8. Documentation	____	____	____	
9. Viewpoint	____	____	____	
10. Mood	____	____	____	
11. Depth, Weight, Intensity	____	____	____	
12. Taboo Avoidance	____	____	____	
13. Readability	____	____	____	
14. Organization	____	____	____	
15. Main Title, Subtitle	____	____	____	
16. Chapter Titles and Subtitles	____	____	____	
17. Beginning	____	____	____	
18. Middle	____	____	____	
19. Ending	____	____	____	
				____
Style & Technique				
20. Style	____	____	____	
21. Writing Technique	____	____	____	
22. Use of Basic Writing Principles	____	____	____	
23. Word Preferences	____	____	____	
24. Language Usage	____	____	____	
25. Polishing and Rewriting	____	____	____	
Total Scores				____

Scoring Key:

		7=Well above average
1=Very low	4=Below average	8=Excellent
2=Low	5=Low average	9=Superior
3=Well below average	6=High average	10=Truly exceptional

HOW TO USE THE EXPOSITORY-WRITING MANUSCRIPT SCORECARD

1. ***Make photo copies of the form provided*** on page 37. This will allow repeated use of the form. Be sure a blank copy is kept on file as a photo-copy master.
2. ***Evaluate the manuscript under consideration, assigning a score for each criterion.*** Grade each of the twenty-five factors on a score range of 1-10, with 1 being low, 5 being average, and 10 being very high. The following grade scale may be used or adapted:

1 = Very low	6 = High average
2 = Low	7 = Well above average
3 = Well below average	8 = Excellent
4 = Below average	9 = Superior
5 = Low average	10 = Truly exceptional

   Write the score for each category in the *Score* column to the left of the weighted scores. Use the above evaluation criteria explanations as guidelines.
3. ***Customize the scorecard if desired.*** The importance of each criterion may be perceived differently by various publishing companies or individual authors. The scorecard can be easily customized by changing the relative weights of the various criteria.
4. ***Determine the weighted score for each category.*** Multiply the *weight* times the *score* for each category, writing the result in the *Weighted Score* column.
5. ***Total the Weighted Score column.*** This will give a numerical evaluation for the manuscript which can be compared against other manuscript evaluations to aid in selecting the best manuscripts available or to indicate the strengths and weaknesses of the manuscript being evaluated.
6. ***Set up a scorecard program on computer for easy evaluation.*** Reproduce the scorecard on a spreadsheet program so that evaluation results can be easily entered

and printed out. If several evaluations are obtained for each manuscript, additional columns can be added to the right, and the individual evaluations can be programmed to add together into a grand total.

Greater value will be added if you take each of the criteria on pages 41 through 53 and put them into a spreadsheet program so you can evaluate each separate item individually. It is evaluation at that level that will help you discover the corrections you should make that will significantly raise the quality of your manuscript.

Expository-Writing Manuscript Scorecard Example

Title ______________________________

Author ____________________ Ms. # __________

Evaluated by____________________Date __________

Criteria	Weight	Score	Weighted Score	Average
Subject & Audience				
1. Significance of Subject	3	6	18	
2. Motivational Impact	3	10	30	
3. Reader Demand	3	4	12	
4. Reader Benefits	3	9	27	
5. Audience Definition	3	8	24	
6. Author's Credentials	2	9	18	
		46	129	7.7
Content & Structure				
7. Research	3	4	12	
8. Documentation	3	3	9	
9. Viewpoint	1	6	6	
10. Mood	1	7	7	
11. Depth, Weight, Intensity	2	5	10	
12. Taboo Avoidance	1	7	7	
13. Readability	3	9	27	
14. Organization	3	7	21	
15. Main Title, Subtitle	3	3	9	
16. Chapter Titles and Subtitles	3	3	9	
17. Beginning	2	7	14	
18. Middle	2	5	10	
19. Ending	2	8	16	
		74	157	5.7
Style & Technique				
20. Style	3	8	24	
21. Writing Technique	3	6	18	
22. Use of Basic Writing Principles	3	7	21	
23. Word Preferences	2	7	14	
24. Language Usage	2	6	12	
25. Polishing and Rewriting	3	6	18	
		40	107	6.7
Total Scores		160	393	6.4

Scoring Key:

1=Very low
2=Low
3=Well below average
4=Below average
5=Low average
6=High average
7=Well above average
8=Excellent
9=Superior
10=Truly exceptional

EXPOSITORY WRITING CRITERIA

1. Significance of Subject

- a significant contribution to existing knowledge
- a significant addition to past and present understanding
- contains one or more compelling unique features not easily available elsewhere
- contains striking ideas not previously thought or expressed
- has a fresh new approach, insight, or angle
- is unusual in quality and content
- is not just a rehash of previously assembled information
- meets a widespread need
- answers questions, deals with significant problems
- effectively fulfills one of the *seven purposes of writing:*
    - to inform
    - to persuade
    - to awaken thought
    - to convince
    - to rebuke
    - to entertain
    - to share personal insights
- contains something unique that makes the book worth publishing
- reflects a sound, healthy philosophy
- the book speaks for itself; no outside explanation is needed

2. Motivational Impact

- will cause people to change their minds
- will cause people to feel strong emotions
- will cause people to take action
- will cause people to share their own thoughts with others
- will cause people to alter their attitudes or character
- will cause people's minds to think, their hearts to love, their whole beings to act on valid principles
- will cheer the reader, renew his self-confidence, and renew his faith and vision

3. Reader Demand

- the content has widespread appeal
- is a useful treatment of a widely discussed topic
- reaches a broad readership audience
- fills a well-defined need
- treats materials which will be regarded as significant by the targeted audience

4. Reader Benefits

- includes a strong reader "take away" of conspicuous benefits
- does not leave the reader with a "so what?" feeling
- leads the reader to discovery
- readers will consider the book to be of above-average value
- readers will perceive the book to be a source of information which they can use and feel to be beneficial

5. Audience Definition

- The targeted audience is carefully identified by:
    - gender
    - age group
    - education level
    - financial status
    - prior knowledge of the subject
    - interest level
    - need for the material
    - reading level
- the targeted audience is accessible through established marketing channels
- the targeted audience is defined as broadly as possible
- realistic consideration has been given to cross-over markets

6. Author's Credentials

- the author has authority, ability to write, and experience in the subject area
- the author's writing represents "expert knowledge" on the subject

- the author has achieved public recognition for his work on the subject
- the author has taught or spoken widely on the subject
- the author has the authority of successful accomplishment in the subject area
- the author is in touch with new ideas, methods, materials, and public taste on the subject

7. Research

- is complete and thorough
- the book is based on an abundance of useable material
- a significant portion is based on primary research: first-hand information obtained and recorded by the author
- is not just secondary "printed page" research
- is not shallow or superficial research
- is not just a collection of facts or quotations
- is neither overdone nor underdone (is adequate but not overpowering)

8. Documentation

- quotations are accurately recorded and have been carefully proofread by the author
- includes a strong table of contents, bibliography, and index
- proper form is followed for footnotes, endnotes, and bibliography
- points and arguments are fully supported with valid evidence
- doesn't make unsupported statements and assumptions
- avoids irrelevant trivia
- materials used are properly identified as to source
- sufficient material is gathered and documented

9. Viewpoint

- uses one of ***three approaches:***
    - the author is detached, free of emotional involvement, withholds personal opinions, is totally objective
    - the author is alive, sympathetic, in touch, and emotionally tied to the subject, but functions at a distance

- the author is empathetic, writes with a depth of feeling for what others feel on the subject
- is a realistic presentation; points are practical and useable
- is written from a positive approach that dispenses hope and confidence
- is written both to the head and to the heart
- the author is not a know-it-all; he doesn't exalt himself or portray himself as the perfect example

10. Mood

- is upbeat and positive
- the author avoids depressing situations (pessimism, negative viewpoints, loser themes, condemnation without hope, trauma ridden with despair, unresolved conflicts or fears, bickering, antagonism, etc.)
- is scholarly, humorous, inspirational
- is realistic; presents an accurate, positive picture of life
- inspires to positive action
- the mood is consistently maintained throughout the book

11. Depth, Weight, Intensity

- focuses increasingly on the subject (broad to narrow, general to specific, distant to close, vague to sharp)
- uses a proper vocabulary level for the targeted audience
- is written to hold the interest of the targeted audience
- is neither too profound nor too light for the targeted audience
- readability is enhanced by anecdotes and personal experiences
- examples and anecdotes are appropriate for the targeted audience and for the subject
- utilizes a concept level appropriate for the targeted audience
- is within the reach and understanding of the targeted audience
- avoids dull language, monotonous repetition of little words

- is mentally exciting and emotionally satisfying copy, written with strong emotional impact
- communicates effectively with the intended reader
- lightens with humor
- uses an appropriate level of thoroughness
- is properly addressed to beginners, intermediates, or advanced readers in the subject-matter area

12. Taboo Avoidance

- avoids worn-out themes (frequently used themes approached from the same angle)
- avoids attitudes out of the past (Victorian innocence, family relationships, minorities, male and female roles, etc.)
- avoids platitudes (trite truisms which give the writing a banal, didactic, pompous quality; outmoded and overused statements)
- avoids historical, emotional or doctrinal biases
- avoids immorality, vulgarity, bad taste, or material which might offend readers
- avoids libelous statements, plagiarism, unauthorized use of protected materials, or the unacknowledged copying of another's research
- avoids unwarranted, undocumented criticism of others
- avoids out-of-date materials, viewpoints, and concepts

13. Readability

- uses good illustrations
- is enhanced by anecdotes
- uses personal experiences to demonstrate concepts
- has sincerity and intensity of purpose
- avoids pomposity and ostentation
- stays on track
- keeps moving forward with fresh new thoughts and insights
- avoids dullness, triteness, dragging flow
- answers questions, deals with real problems
- develops the subject logically
- leads the reader to personal discoveries

14. Organization

- follows a sequential organization:
  - topical
  - chronological
  - logical
  - spatial (geographical)
- follows a clear-cut theme approach:
  - question theme
  - set-of-facts theme
  - adventure
  - problem
  - place
  - biographical
  - inspiration/moral
  - personal opinion
  - doctrinal
- focuses effectively (moves from general to specific, vague to sharp, broad to narrow, distant to close)
- shows evidence of careful outlining and planning

15. Main Title and Subtitle

Main Title:

- is easily pronounced
- is easily understood
- is brief (usually 5 words or less, preferably 2 or 3 words)
- is original
- catches the reader's interest, arrests his attention (jumps off the page)
- is specific, appropriate, not misleading
- is fresh and alive, with color and excitement; not lifeless or limp

Subtitle:

- clearly defines the book's subject, scope and viewpoint
- supplies pertinent information not given in the main title
- doesn't duplicate words from the main title
- promises what the book will deliver
- is slanted towards the reader and the market
- relies on active verbs, concrete "picture" nouns

16. Chapter Titles and Subtitles

Chapter Titles:

- are easily understood
- are specific, clearly explain the contents of the chapter
- maintain balance: chapters are approximately the same length throughout the book
- are parallel in style: all contain (or don't contain) verbs, etc.

Chapter Subtitles:

- are easily understood
- are specific, clearly explain the contents of the section
- maintain balance: chapter sections are approximately the same length throughout the chapter
- are parallel in style: all contain (or don't contain) verbs, etc.

17. Beginning

- "hooks" the reader and claims his/her immediate attention
- begins at a high point of interest and action
- defines the central theme or problem early, grabs the reader
- is intense, has impact
- doesn't introduce too much background in the first sentences
- introduces the topic(s), sets the stage, sets the mood
- extends to the point where the problem or theme is clearly defined
- front matter is thoroughly prepared, including table of contents

18. Middle

- clarifies the author's motivation and reveals how he/she copes with the situation
- begins to fulfill the interesting promises presented in the beginning
- each chapter is a self-contained unit with a clear beginning, middle and end
- chapters end at appropriate places and their endings have the same approximate length and format

- chapters and sub-sections grow logically out of previous materials, but each has a new message, theme or solution to a problem
- chapters are a series of progressive additions, all related to the central theme; they move the theme forward
- each chapter clearly is essential to the overall book

19. Ending

- solves the problem with firm finality
- has emotional impact and "punch"
- is not anticlimactic
- ties up loose ends
- is logical, credible
- pleases, rewards and satisfies the reader, doesn't cheat him/her
- shows how, when, why
- resolves conflicts, draws conclusions, makes projections
- makes the book memorable
- a "clincher" or "twist" at the end clearly answers the reader's question: "so what?"
- stops when the message is over
- ends with a
    - summary
    - challenge
    - projection
    - quotation
    - anecdote
    - thesis
    - punch line

20. Style

- is indicated by the author's selection and arrangement of words—his vocabulary, flow of words, colorful phrases, and general tone
- may be:
    - scholarly
    - homey
    - light and funny
    - heavy and dull
    - anecdotal
    - picturesque
    - formal
    - humorous

- cynical
- flowery
- dignified
- philosophical
- conversational
- carefree
- arduous
- breezy
- preachy
- text-bookish

- reveals the author's personality, life outlook, education, beliefs, ethics, imagination
- is written with natural ease; the author is not self-conscious
- is not imitative of others
- the author has a ready vocabulary
- the author's style is shown in his/her originality, discipline, ability to arouse emotions, and technical mastery of the writer's craft

21. Writing Technique

Modern Style:

- uses terse, efficient prose
- uses tight, careful construction, is to the point
- avoids outdated techniques (long descriptive passages, rambling wordiness)
- uses up-to-date language, themes, outcomes
- avoids outdated slang, expressions and clichés

Sentence usage:

- sentences vary in length and type
- sentences make good sense, are clearly understood and not confusing
- sentences are not choppy, cluttered, nor rambling
- sentences are not long and complicated
- sentences have the most important word near the beginning or end
- run-on sentences are avoided

Paragraph usage:

- sentences follow in logical sequence
- paragraphs vary in length and sentence type
- most paragraphs are less than 125 words in length
- paragraphs have a topic sentence which expresses the central thought

Narrative:

- narrative is kept to a minimum; stories are mostly told through dialogue and description
- the author shows events through his/her characters, doesn't tell the story
- the narrator is a participant, not a bystander

Point of View:

- remains constant throughout the book
- remains either first or third person
- if multiple points of view are used, makes as few shifts as possible
- avoids a "they" viewpoint
- avoids an omniscient all-knowing multiple viewpoint

Objective or Subjective Writing:

- objective writing reports the facts and avoids personal opinions or biases
- subjective writing intentionally reflects the author's personal opinions and biases
- does not shift between the two writing approaches in the book

Flashbacks:

- provide needed background information, clarify or intensify present information
- explain why present situations exist
- don't interrupt current information or spoil the chapter's continuity
- are used with restraint, not overused
- are brief and concise
- are entered and exited with good, easily recognized transitions
- don't raise questions concerning the main chronology

Transitions:

- connect words, ideas, and events smoothly
- move characters from place to place, time to time, or emotion to emotion
- serve as a shortcut, moving from "here" to "there" fast
- concepts are linked together with carryover features

- transition words are clearly positioned at beginnings of sentences which contain little detail so they're easily recognized

Attention to Details:

- no details are left unresolved
- no concepts are left unexplained, undocumented or unaccounted for

Emphasis:

- avoids overuse of exclamation points, italics, underlined words, words in all-capital letters

Overworked Words:

- absence of *amateur and overworked words:*
  - very
  - have
  - had
  - so
  - seems
  - then
  - but
  - just
  - oh
- absence of *overworked adverbs:*
  - almost
  - actually
  - practically
  - naturally
  - virtually
  - suddenly
  - really
  - absolutely
  - probably
  - obviously
  - undoubtedly
  - definitely
  - positively
- absence of *trite phrases:*
  - as you can see
  - it goes without saying
  - as you must know
  - there is reason to believe that
- is not redundant—needless extra words which restate what's already said have been eliminated
- is free from clichés and colloquialisms
- is free from anachronisms (people, places, things and words used out of their proper time or setting)

22. Use of Basic Writing Principles

Clarity:

- the ideas are clear
- all parts of the ideas are expressed
- the ideas cannot be misunderstood

Unity:

- all parts are related
- all parts contribute to clear, overall ideas

- the theme, point of view, mood and tense are constant, consistent and unchanging

Coherence:

- all parts are arranged in logical order
- all relationships are clearly expressed

Conciseness:

- all ideas are expressed with brevity and economy

Emphasis:

- the ideas are arranged to show their relative importance
- key words are positioned at the beginning or end of sentences
- key ideas are positioned at the beginning or end of paragraphs

Interest:

- ideas are expressed effectively so they attract and hold reader interest
- ideas are of sufficient quality that they merit reader interest

23. Word Preferences

- prefers familiar words, not unfamiliar ones
- prefers Saxon words, not Romance words (uses English or German rather than French, Italian, Spanish, Portuguese)
- prefers nouns and verbs, not adjectives and adverbs
- prefers short words, not long ones
- prefers concrete words, not general ones
- prefers single words, not phrases
- prefers simple sentences, not complex ones
- prefers active voice, not passive voice
- prefers picture nouns, not non-image nouns
- prefers action verbs, not forms of the verb "to be"
- prefers action verbs, not adverb-verb combinations
- prefers action verbs, not inactive verbs
- prefers short paragraphs, not long paragraphs
- prefers original words and phrases, not trite ones
- prefers past tense, not past perfect tense
- prefers the specific, not the general
- prefers the concrete, not the abstract

24. Language Usage

- uses correct grammar
- uses correct punctuation
- uses correct spelling
- uses correct structure, form and technique
- uses lively and varied vocabulary
- uses words that create moods through their rhythm and inner sounds and through the images they invoke
- uses words that make interesting and pleasing sounds (***assonance:*** resemblance of sounds in words and syllables, especially vowels; repetition of vowels without repetition of consonants (as in *holy* and *story*); used as an alternative to rhyme in verse; ***alliteration:*** the repetition of initial consonant sounds in two or more neighboring words or syllables (as *thr*eatening *thr*ongs, *w*ild and *w*ooly); ***onomatopoeia:*** the naming of a thing or action by a vocal imitation of the sound associated with it (as *buzz, hiss*); the use of words whose sound suggests the sense of the statement)
- uses show-and-tell words that paint pictures through the imagery of metaphors and similes
- avoids flowery, sentimental, preachy, and unnecessary words

25. Polishing and Rewriting

- the complete absence of careless errors gives clear evidence of extensive polishing and thorough proofreading
- superfluous words have been deleted
- involved sentences have been simplified
- the grammar, spelling, punctuation and word accuracy have been corrected
- the manuscript has professional tone, sparkle and style
- spelling has been corrected; computer spell checks and grammar checks have been made
- punctuation has been corrected
- computer keyboarding has been corrected so the book can be typeset from the author's disk
- footnotes, endnotes and bibliographies are uniform in style and follow formats recommended in acceptable style manuals

3

Guidelines for Writing for Children and Teens

INTRODUCTION

One of the most significant problems publishers observe in the hundreds of manuscripts for children and teens which they receive each year is the lack of careful market and age-group identification. Most authors fail to properly identify the exact age group they are writing for and the type of book they need to be writing for that age of reader.

In this chapter, a suggested classification system for writing for children is presented, under the title ***Junior Book Field*** (*Books for Children Ages 2 - 12*). Four types of books are suggested: *picture books, picture story books, easy-to-read books,* and *'tween-age books.* Under the title ***Teen Book Field***, three types of books are discussed: *teen books, teenage romance books,* and *hi / lo books.*

The second very obvious problem publishers observe is that many manuscripts for young age groups use vocabularies which are far too advanced for most children in the age-group targeted by the plot and art work. Books for six-year-olds shouldn't be filled with four-syllable words!

To help alleviate this problem, lists of words typically taught in each grade from one to six are presented. These are valuable lists which allow authors to check the vocabulary they have utilized in their manuscripts against word lists which are accepted and utilized by educators across the country.

Obviously, books which support educators' teaching efforts through the choice of words utilized will have far greater support from teachers than those books which lie far beyond the skill level of the typical child for whom the books' plots and character development are targeted. Experienced authors writing for young children know that teacher acceptance and support for what they write makes a vast difference in the sales of their books!

The chapter ends with a list of general characteristics of good writing for young teenagers.

JUNIOR BOOK FIELD
(Books for Children Ages 2-12)

1. Picture Books

- ***Ages 2-5***
- 50-500 words
- Little text, pictures on every page

2. Picture Story Books

- ***Ages 4-9***
- 500-2,500 words
- To be read by an adult to the child
- Must have a definite plot line
- Main character must achieve a definite goal, undergo a significant change
- Needs lots of story action
- Should avoid adult whims (plays on words, too-complex-situations, erudite language, adult-level poetry)

3. Easy-to-Read Books

- ***Ages 6-9***
- 500-2,000 words (1,000-1,500 words preferred)
- To be read by the child
- Must be fun to read
- Needs a lively plot featuring adventure, mystery or humor
- Main character must achieve a definite goal, undergo a significant change

4. 'Tween-age Books

- ***Ages 8-12***
- 5,000 to 40,000 words
- Main character has a definite personality with several distinct character traits
- Typical topics:
    - Stories of yesterday, today, and tomorrow
    - Mysteries and adventure
    - Facts and fiction about people and places
    - Current events: conservation, ecology, air pollution, space exploration
    - Familiar things: families, animals, sports

TEEN BOOK FIELD
(Books for Youth Ages 12-19)

1. Teen Books

- ***Ages 12-16*** (possibly 10-15 for advanced readers)
- Characters are fully developed, as in adult books
- Characters strive to understand themselves; they explore and experiment
- This age group wants stories that are fun to read
- Popular subjects:
  - suspense tales
  - science fiction
  - biographies
- Sometimes deal with the stark *realities of life:*
  - divorce
  - unmarried pregnancy
  - alcoholism
  - child abuse
  - mental illness
- Sometimes deal with *social issues:*
  - women's rights
  - status of the underprivileged
  - civil disturbances
  - politics
  - the new morality
  - idealistic new worlds
- Underlying values: reflect a sound, healthy philosophy, something that makes the book worth publishing:
  - information
  - a message

2. Teenage Romance Books

- Sees life from a girl's viewpoint
- Shouldn't preach or be condescending
- Portrays teenage concerns:
  - lows and highs
  - fear of rejection
  - life's uncertainties
  - adolescence

  - physical and emotional changes
- Common problems: weak characterizations, unrealistic plots

3. Hi/Lo Books

- High-interest books requiring low reading-level skills, for readers with reading problems
- Stories must be fast-paced, with lots of dialogue
- Deal with realistic contemporary problems
- Often emphasize ethnic groups and backgrounds

THE IMPORTANCE OF USING APPROPRIATE VOCABULARY WHEN WRITING CHILDREN'S BOOKS

Authors who write for elementary-school-aged children need to align their writing with the vocabulary that young children have learned or are learning in their schools. Presented below are lists of words commonly taught for each age level in popular curricula used nation-wide for teaching reading in grades one through six.

FIRST GRADE VOCABULARY

A
a
above
air
always
an
and
animals
around
at

B
back
bad
bake
bear
birds
black
blew
blue
born
brother
brown

C
can
care
cat
cheese
city
come
community
cook
cookies
country

D
dad
did
do
dog
down
drink

E
earth
eat
ecology

F
family
favorite
find
fish
food
friends

G
garden
get
go
good
grandma
grandpa
green
ground

H
have
help
his
house

I
I
if
in
insects
is
it

J
job

K
kind
know

L
left
like
little
live
long
look
lunch

M
many
mix
mom
moon
more
moth
mother
mouse
much
my

N
need
neighbor
neighborhood
no
noodles
not

O
of
old
on
out

P
parade
people
pizza
place
plants
play
pond

R
ready
red
rescue

S
said
same
save
saw
school
see
share
she
silly
sister
size
sleep
snail
some
soup
special
splash
spring
store
storm
street
sun

FIRST GRADE VOCABULARY
(Continued)

T

taste
the
them
then
there
they
this
to
together
too
town
trash

U

under
up

V

vegetable
very

W

water
went
what
when
where
wild
will
wind
winter
with
work
write

Y

yellow
yes
you
your

Z

zoo

See, also, the ***Dolch Reading System First Grade "Sight Words"*** listed on pages 72-73.

SECOND GRADE VOCABULARY

A
action
active
adventure
alarm
Alaska
alligator
amazing
angrily
athlete
audition
awesome

B
baggy
balance
ballerina
bamboo
beliefs
bloom
blotchy
blubber
bough

C
cabinet
carnival
cartilage
champion
chess
chilly
choir
clever
clip
clipper ship
clock
coast
commands
continent
costume
creature
croquet
culture
custom
customer

D
darting
decision
den
diagonally
dinosaur
disguise
duplicated

E
eel
enemies
energy
entertain
everyone
exciting
exercise

F
fabric
fashion
favorite
feast
feat
Ferris wheel
fierce
figurehead
fireplace
fossils
furry

G
gather
gear
geyser
GI
gill
gooey
grabbed
graduate
grind
grumbled
guide

H
hammer
harness
hatch
haunches
headdresses
healthy
hilarious
hoisted
howl
hurricane

I
Iceland
icy
ignored
imaginary
impressed
island

J
jacket
jaunty

K
karate
knife

L
language
learn
lobster

M
maize
mast
meadow
medal
medusa
midday
mime
miniature
minisubmarine
motor
muscles
mussel

N
neighborhood
nerve

O
Olympics
outfit
oxygen

P
pajamas
partners
patch
perform
pickup
plump
polar bear
porthole
pounced
pound

SECOND GRADE VOCABULARY
(Continued)

practice
practicing
prance
president
pretend
protect
proud
provisions
prow
Pueblo people
puffer fish
puffin

R

rarely
record
recycle
reed
reef
refrigerated
remind
reporter
rescue
respect
robot

S

sacrifice
saw
school
scowl
sea anemone
sea urchin
seaweed
self-defense
senior
sense
shield
shoved
signals
silent
ski
slink
smug
snout
soar
soccer
sole
sow
sparkle
sparkling
spike
sports
stalk
steam
stitch
story
storyteller
stuffed
supermarket
surprise
survive
swamp

T

tadpole
team
terrible
thief
thinnest
together
traditional
train
trek
trip
tuna

V

Viet Nam
volunteers

W

warm
weather
welder
wheelchair
whispered
winter
wire
world
worried

Y

yarn
yeast

See, also, the ***Dolch Reading System Second Grade "Sight Words"*** listed on pages 74-75.

THIRD GRADE VOCABULARY

A
accordion
acre
adjustment
adopt
adoption
agency
alphabet
American Sign Language
amount
ancestors
apologize
asphalt
astronaut
attention
aviation

B
backgrounds
bacteria
bamboo
barges
barnstormer
bok choy
bronco
brood
bueno
bunions
burrow

C
Cajun
camouflage
Cantonese
carbon dioxide
chariot
childhood
chorizo
chuckle
Cinco de Mayo
citrus
clasped
comb
comforting
communicate
compete
con huevos
conflict
convenience
conversation
coop
coral
corral
corrido
creative
Creole

D
dead zone
dependent
devices
dialect
dim
dragon
drainage

E
emperor
endangered species
environment
exactly
exasperation
experiment
explained
extra-terrestrial

F
fantastico
festival
fiesta
folklorico
fried rice
frijoles
frond
fungi
furrow

G
gestures
glider
grains
gravel

H
Haitian
harvest
headwaters
Hebrew
hologram
honesty
humus

I
independent
ingredient
interrupt
interview
iridescent

K
kernel
kibbutz

L
laboratory
language
language
larva
latex
legend
lichen
limousine
linen

M
mariachi
mediators
memories
messages
meteor
mission
Mississippi
migrant
models
moisture
mulch
muttered
muy bien
muy malo

N
native
noticed

O
observe
orchard
orchid
organic
oxygen

THIRD GRADE VOCABULARY
(Continued)

P

panda
pantry
papas fritas
pastime
patience
peer
pesticides
piñata
pod
polite
pollutants
pomegranate
porcelain
possibility
powered
preciosa
privileges
produce
province
prune

Q

quilt

R

rafts
recipe
recycling
reduce
refuel
register
renewable
resolve
resource
respect
restless
reuse
rice paper
rodeo
rudeness

S

samples
sap
sassy
satisfied
shelter
shoot
shortening
shy
signal
similar
simulated
skiffs
soak
society
solar system
solar-powered
space station
Sri Lanka
stalk
step family
stethoscope
stranded
stubborn
stunt
swirling
symbol

T

tadpoles
tamales
teased
temple
topsoil
tortilla
totem
totem pole
tousled
traditions
trampoline

V

vacant
vaqueros
venture
violence

W

walkway
weathered
weightlessness

FOURTH GRADE VOCABULARY

A

access
accidentally
achieve
acid rain
admire
adobe
advertise
aerial
agreement
airwaves
aloha
alternative
annexation
apartment
appearance
appreciative
approval
archaeology
arroyo
artificial
arts
attitude
attract

B

background
basalt
battery
Bedouin
bill
botanist
broadcast
buggy
burrow
business
bustling
butte

C

cab
cable car
calabash
calamity
caldera
cause
center
centipede
ceremony
certainty
challenge
chamber
character
characteristic
coalition
committee
communicate
community
commuter
compete
complained
concern
confidently
conserve
constitution
contributor
convenient
countryside
creative
culture
curiosity
custom
customs

D

demonstrate
design
device
dialogue
diversity
dormant
downtown
drive-in
drought
dune
Dust Bowl

E

edit
efficient
emotion
empower
endangered
endure
environmental
epicenter
erosion
evaporate
excavate
exodus
express
extinct

F

factory
fault
festival
fiber
fire escape
formation
fossil
fuel

G

garble
gasoline
generation
geology
gesture
Great
Depression
grounded
guide
guilt
gullies

H

habitat
harvesting
heritage
highway
hinalea
Hopi
horsepower
hula

I

ignore
illusion
image
immigrant
incinerator
industrial park
industry
influence
input
inter-
dependence
inventor
irrigation
issue

L

landing
landlord
larvae
lava
lore

FOURTH GRADE VOCABULARY
(Continued)

M

magnitude
main
manufacturing
media
mental
mesa
message
migrant
migration
mimic
mineral
missionary
moisture
monarchy
motel
motif
motivation
mutter
mysterious

N

Navajo
navigator
neighborhood

O

oasis
obvious
offshore
opinion
optical illusion
ordinary
outrigger
overcrowding

P

paleontologist
patent
pattern
perch
pillar
plantation
plate tectonics
poi
polite
politics
pollinate
pollutant
pollution
population
potential
prairie
prejudice
preserve
pride
product
pueblo

Q

quality

R

realistic
recharge
recycled
regretted
reinforce
reputation
respect
responsible
Richter scale
rodent
roots
rural

S

saguaro
scarce
sediment
sedimentary
segment
segregated
seismograph
seismologist
self-confidence
serendipity
shame
sign
skill
skyline
skyscraper
slogan
spelunking
squall
stalactite
stalagmite
stoop
story
straight-forward
strata
streetcar
struggle
suburb
subway
superfluous
support
suspicion
symbol
synagogue

T

taro
technology
tenant
texture
throng
tourist
tradition
transform
translate
trolley
tropical

U

urban
utility

V

value
victory
visual
voice
volunteer

W

waterway
windbreak

Y

yucca

Z

Zuni

FIFTH GRADE VOCABULARY

A
a cappella
abacus
abandon
abruptly
abstract
accessory
aerobics
allegro
allowance
amateur
ambitious
andante
android
animated
animator
animatronics
annual
anthem
apologize
architect
assemble
attend
automatons
awkward

B
barrier
binary code
brilliant
budget
bunt
byte

C
camaraderie
cassava
celebrity
cello
championship
chord
circulation
citizen
civilization
coda
commitment
companionship
competition
complexion
compose
composite
composition
concentration
conduct
conservatory
constructive
coordination
corps
counselor
creation
crescendo
critic
crisis
crude
culinary
culminating
culture
cyclist

D
data
decathlon
dedicated
dedication
deferred
defiant
degree
delicious
delirious
demanding
deprived
dignified
discharged
discouraged
discrimination
disdainful
domestic
donate
dribble

E
eavesdrop
elegant
eliminate
elongated
energy
entangle
enthusiastic
epidemic
exercise
exhibition
exile
expectation
expedition
expressive
extensive
extermination

F
feasible
federal
fiction
field
flexibility
fluorescent
foul
freestyle

G
gadgets
gallery
generate
geometrical
gesture
gripper
guavas

H
harmony
hesitate
hotline
husbandry
hypochondriac

I
imitation
influence
ingredient
inherited
injustices
innumerable
input
instill
instinct
investigative

J
judgment

K
kernel
kilobyte
knack

L
league
lofty
lynched
lyrical

FIFTH GRADE VOCABULARY
(Continued)

M

marathon
marine biologist
marmalade
media
megabyte
memoir
mermaid
migrants
mild
minstrel
minuet
mold
movement
mural
muscle

N

needy
nutrient

O

obstetrician
Olympic games
opera
oppression
oral
ordeal
output

P

panel
paraplegic
parish
participant
particular
partitions
passive
patronage
pentathlon
pervasive
pitch
pitfalls
play-offs
poll
portion
portrait
posture
precipitate
proclamation
professional
progress
promotion
protest
provocative

Q

quartet

R

race
rancid
rarity
recital
recognition
recruiting
reflex
rehabilitated
relay
reluctantly
remarkable
rescue
researcher
resource
revelation
rhythm
rhythmic
ridicule
roster
rotate
routed
routines

S

sacred
scavengers
scouting
self-esteem
Senegalese
sensors
shot
sluggers
solitude
somersault
spellbound
spice
spotters
spring
sprinter
squad
stalagmites
steroids
stress
substitute
subtle
supercilious
supervise
survival
symphony

T

tasty
teamwork
technician
technique
three-dimensional
tolerant
tradition
transplant
triathlon
trophy
troupe
tumblers
tumultuous

U

unique
unschooled

V

versatility
version
vibrato
victory
victuals
vision
volunteer
volunteers

W

workable

Y

yarn

SIXTH GRADE VOCABULARY

A

abundance
acidity
acquit
aliens
allegiance
alteration
ancestors
artisans
assay
assimilate
assume
auction
avalanche

B

bantam
bard
barter
bauble
blacklist
boatswain
bonds
boycott
brilliant
brooding

C

camcorder
Caucasians
censored
ceremony
circumstances
claim
clinic
clutch
combustion
commenced
commend
commotion
complicated
component
compress
conceal
conductor
conference
congress
consent
conserve
contract
converse
cooperation
corridors
cultivate
cultural
culture
cylinder

D

daylight saving time
deceit
defective
deformity
deity
delirium
deposit
detector
determination
dignity
dilapidated
dioxide
discipline
discourage
dissatisfied
dissected
diversity
drought

E

ecology
ecosystem
elegy
element
embedded
endorphins
engrave
enrich
environment
envy
evacuation
evidence
exhibition
expedition
expertise
exploit
exposure
expression

F

fabricated
fatal
fatigue
feature
feeble
fetch
finances
fisticuffs
flamethrower
flexible
flotilla
formula
fossil
foster
fuel
fuse

G

generalized
geology
gerry-mandering
gorge
granite
grub
guidance

H

heritage
hoax
hold
horizon
horn
hysteria

I

identity
immigrant
immune
inappropriate
industrialized
ingenious
inscription
integral
integrate
inter-generational
interlocking
internal
interned
interview
intricate
invasion
issues

SIXTH GRADE VOCABULARY
(Continued)

J

Jericho
journalist
justice

K

kaleidoscope
kinship

L

limitations
links
litter

M

manslaughter
marvelous
matriarchy
Maya
meditate
mentally
microorganism
migration
mineral
miniature
multitude
mythical

N

native
Native American
natural
nausea
navigation
neon
nimble
nucleus
nugget
nutritious

O

obsidian
offshore drilling
opposition
oracular
origin

P

palisade
paralyze
parchment
pernicious
persuade
petrified wood
phenomenon
physical
plight
poacher
pollutant
Polynesia
portrays
positive
potential
prairie
precipitation
predator
prejudice
principles
privacy
prohibited
properties
proportions

Q

quarrelsome
quartz
querulous
quest

R

racism
random
rapid
ratify
recreation
refugees
regalia
regulate
relative
relocate
reservation
residents
resources
retarded
revealed
richness
rock hound
rollicking
rotate

S

sacred
sanctuary
sarcasm
sassy
scabbard
scoff
segregate
sidewheeler
signify
silage
sinister
sleek
solar
sounded
speculate
spiral
spoon
standard time
status
stimulate
stranded
strenuous
stronghold
studio
subcontinent
sulfur
summon
supernova
support
surfeit
swirled
symmetry

T

teamwork
technical
telepathy
theory
tradition
traitors
treaty
trek
tribe
truce
tundra
typical

U

unique
uniquely
unreliable

V

valor
veranda
vigorous
violation
vulnerable

SIXTH GRADE VOCABULARY
(Continued)

W	Y
whirlpool	yard
willingness	yardarm
winch	Yucatan
wistfully	

The following list of "sight words" identifies 220 words which young children are expected to know before they are regarded as "readers." They are part of the Dolch reading system which has been in use in many American schools for several decades.

DOLCH READING SYSTEM
FIRST GRADE "SIGHT WORDS"

A

a
about
again
airplane
all
am
an
and
apple
are
as
at
away

B

baby
back
ball
be
bed
big
birthday
black
blue
boat
bow-wow
boy
but

C

cake
call
came
can
cap
car
Christmas
come
cookies
could
cow
cowboy

D

daddy
did
dinner
dish
do
dog
down

E

eat

F

farm
father
find
fine
fish
for
from
fun
funny

G

get
girl
give
go
good
goodbye
green

H

had
happy
has
have
he
help
her
here
hide
him
his
home
house
how

I

I
in
is
it

J

jump
just

K

kitten
know

L

laugh
let
like
little
long
look

M

make
man
many
may
me
mitten
morning
mother
Mr.
must
my

N

near
new

DOLCH READING SYSTEM FIRST GRADE "SIGHT WORDS" (Continued)

night
no
not
now

O

of
oh
on
one

P

party
pie
play
pretty
puppy
put

R

rabbit
ran
red
ride
run

S

said
sat
saw
see
she
show
sleep
so
some
something
soon
splash
stop
surprise

T

table
take
thank
that
the
them
then
there
they
this
to
too
toy
tree
two

U

up
us

W

walk
want
was
water
way
we
went
were
what
when
where
white
who
will
wish
with
work

Y

yellow
yes
you
your

See, also, the ***First Grade Vocabulary*** words listed on pages 59-60.

The following list of "sight words" identifies 220 words which young children are expected to know before they are regarded as "readers." They are part of the Dolch reading system which has been in use in many American schools for several decades.

DOLCH READING SYSTEM
SECOND GRADE "SIGHT WORDS"

A

a
about
after
again
all
always
am
an
and
any
are
around
as
ask
at
ate
away

B

be
because
been
before
best
better
big
black
black
blue
both
bring
brown
but
buy
by

C

call
came
can
carry
clean
cold
come
could
cut

D

did
do
does
don't
done
down
draw
drink

E

eat
eight
every

F

fall
fast
find
first
five
fly
for
forget
found
four
full
funny

G

gave
give
go
goes
going
good
got
green
grow

H

had
has
have
he
help
her
here
him
his
hold
hot
how
hurt

I

I
if
in
into
is
it
its

J

jump
just

K

keep
kind
know

L

laugh
let
light
like
little
live

DOLCH READING SYSTEM SECOND GRADE "SIGHT WORDS" (Continued)

long
look

M

made
make
many
may
me
much
must
my
myself

N

never
new
no
not
now

O

of
off
old
on
once
one
only
open
or
our
out
own

P

pick
play
please
pretty
pull
put

R

ran
read
red
ride
right
round
run

S

said
saw
say
see
seven
shall
she
show
sing
sit
six
sleep
small
so
some
soon
stop

T

take
tell
ten
thank
that
the
their
them
then
there
these
they
think
this
those
three
to
today
together
too
try
two

U

under
up
upon
us
use

V

very

W

walk
want
was
we
well
were
what
when
where
which
white
who
why
will
wish
with
work
would
write

Y

yellow
yes
you
your

See, also, the ***Second Grade Vocabulary*** words listed on pages 61-62.

SUGGESTIONS FOR EFFECTIVE WRITING FOR YOUNG TEENAGERS

- The protagonist should be as old or slightly older than the targeted-market age group (youth want to be bigger, stronger, older)
- Adults are kept to a minimum; characters receive as little adult assistance as possible
- Characters have individuality; they are not cast in predetermined roles
- Characters have a convincing background; they are life-like
- Characters are able to fight for their goals without whining or self-pity
- Characters have problems suitable to their years
- Stories of courage, daring, and exploration are always popular
- Does not perpetuate tired, stereotyped images (sex and age depictions)
- Subjects are intriguing; they arouse curiosity

4

Writing to Meet Publishers' Needs

INTRODUCTION

When an author submits a manuscript to a publisher for publication consideration, he is actually (1) inviting the publisher to make a sizeable financial investment and (2) seeking to establish an ongoing working relationship with that publisher.

In some ways, an author-publisher arrangement is like a marriage—it must be based on compatibility, mutual interests and objectives, cooperation, courtesy, trust, and a host of other personal-relationship qualities.

Authors who want to see their books in print must learn to write manuscripts in which publishers will be willing to invest. Every publisher has certain “must” criteria an incoming manuscript must meet to be given serious publication scrutiny.

But the more challenging requirements for publication lie in the publisher’s “want” criteria. Almost every publisher is seeking to produce books of good literary quality. Some seek to inform, others to inspire and motivate, still others to provide social commentary, and others seek to entertain. But underlying these literary objectives are the hard financial realities. They must realize a profit. They must meet the expectations of their shareholders. They must “run a tight ship” and maintain solvency.

Many times authors are almost oblivious to these needs. This chapter is written to provide authors with a basic understanding of the financial realities of the manuscript selection process, and of the implications of such factors as book length and format, production timing, production costs, product life, break-even requirements, return-on-investment necessities, and sales and profit potential.

In this chapter, various dollar and time figures have been supplied for illustrative purposes. The amounts supplied would be representative of the needs of a rather small publishing house; larger companies would of course have substantially larger expectations.

MANUSCRIPT SELECTION SCORECARD

Title____________________ Author ____________________

Criteria	Weight	Score	Weighted Score
***MUST* CRITERIA**			
1. Legal Clearance	Go / No Go_______		
2. Ecclesiastical Compatibility	Go / No Go_______		
3. Language Suitability	Go / No Go_______		
4. Publishing Domain	Go / No Go_______		
***WANT* CRITERIA**			
1. Sales Potential	10	______	_______
2. Profit Potential	10	______	_______
3. Return on Investment	9	______	_______
4. Break-even Target	9	______	_______
5. Subject Popularity	8	______	_______
6. Message Strength and Uniqueness	8	______	_______
7. Risk Factor	8	______	_______
8. Production Costs	8	______	_______
9. Retail Price	8	______	_______
10. Product Life	8	______	_______
11. Market Compatibility	7	______	_______
12. Market Crossover Potential	7	______	_______
13. Advertising, Marketing, Promotion	7	______	_______
14. Quality of Writing	6	______	_______
15. Author Stature and Participation	6	______	_______
16. Production Timing	5	______	_______
17. Book Format	4	______	_______
18. Book Length	4	______	_______
19. Editorial Plan Compatibility	3	______	_______
20. Other Product Relationships	2	______	_______
Total Scores		______	_______

Scoring Key:

1=Very low	4=Below average	7=Well above average
2=Low	5=Low average	8=Excellent
3=Well below average	6=High average	9=Superior
		10=Truly exceptional

PUBLISHERS' MANUSCRIPT SELECTION CRITERIA

Must Criteria

1. Legal Clearance

- The manuscript is free of unlawful material, including libelous statements, slander, and plagiarized materials.
- Permission has been obtained in writing for the use of copyrighted materials which exceed "fair use."
- The manuscript is free of any materials which could engender litigation or other legal action against the author and/or the publisher.

2. Ecclesiastical Compatibility (if the publisher has a religious affiliation)

- The manuscript is compatible with the doctrinal perspectives of the publisher's religious affiliation.
- The manuscript is not critical, in its overall tone or message, of the leadership, practices, history, doctrine, policies, or other aspects of the publisher's religious affiliation.
- The manuscript does not utilize language, terminology, or theological concepts which are not commonly recognized, understood, and accepted by well-informed readers of the publisher's religious affiliation.

3. Language Suitability

- The manuscript does not utilize swear words, gutter language, or blasphemous statements.
- The manuscript does not contain pornographic materials or explicit descriptions of sexual experiences.

4. Publishing Domain

- The manuscript subject has not been declared to be outside the firm's present publishing domain. It is compatible with the type of books which the publisher successfully produces and markets.

Want Criteria

1. Sales Potential
- The product has potential to become a "best seller" in its field.
- More than 4,000* copies of the book can be sold in the first six months.
- More than 8,000* copies of the book can be sold in the first twelve months.

2. Profit Potential
- At estimated sales levels, the product has the potential to yield at least twelve percent* net profit during the first six months.
- At estimated sales levels, the product has the potential to yield at least fifteen percent* net profit during its product life cycle.

3. Return on Investment
- The product, at estimated sales levels, will yield at least a twelve percent* return on investment.

4. Break-even Target
- Sales for the product will reach the break-even point within three months.*

5. Subject Popularity
- The subject matter is of considerable interest to a significantly large potential audience which has been specifically identified.
- The subject matter is a useful treatment of a widely discussed topic, has widespread appeal, and fills a well-defined consumer need.

6. Message Strength and Uniqueness
- The book has one or more compelling unique features which are not easily available elsewhere.
- The book fulfills a clearly defined consumer need, desire or interest.

---

* Quantities, percents, and periods of time will vary with each publisher's scheduling, pricing, size of staff, market, advertising, etc.

- The book's subject matter corresponds to areas which are generally accepted and purchased by consumers in the target market(s).
- No competitors' products will have negative impact on the salability of the product in the foreseeable future.

7. Risk Factor

- There is no significant risk of the product being "unsaleable."
- The initial printing of the book will not require production of more than a one-year supply to be manufactured at an economically feasible rate.
- The book is free of distracting elements (poor language, extreme theories, strong prejudices or biases, or other author idiosyncrasies) which might offend readers.
- The book will not in any way draw negative comment nor criticism to the company.

8. Production Costs

- The manuscript text will be provided by the author on computer disks compatible with the company's existing typesetting equipment.
- Editing costs to prepare the manuscript for publication will not exceed budgeted costs for a manuscript of the book's length.
- The manuscript will not require more than normal typesetting corrections.
- The book can be produced in-house, on company equipment, and with existing personnel.
- The book will not require excessive investment for artwork, color separations, etc.

9. Retail Price

- A retail price for the book can be established which will allow adequate return of production expenses, advertising, vendor discounts, return on investment and profit, and will still be within retail price levels generally accepted by the buying public.
- The required retail price for the book will be compatible with list prices for comparable products currently selling in the industry.

10. Product Life

- The book will remain a viable product, generating at least 200* unit sales per month, for at least 36 months after it is published.
- Reprints of the book can be produced without undue difficulty.

11. Market Compatibility

- The book is appropriate for sales in the company's established or targeted market(s).
- The book is compatible with other products being offered in the same market so that advertising and promotion economies can be realized.

12. Market Crossover Potential

- The book has crossover potential; it can be successfully sold in more than one market in which the company is functioning.

13. Advertising, Marketing, Promotion

- The product can be effectively advertised to the targeted market(s).
- An advertising investment of five percent* of the first year's estimated gross sales will be sufficient to generate continuing sales for the book.

14. Quality of Writing

- The book has a strong title (and subtitle, if used).
- The book is technically well written (correct grammar, punctuation, spelling, style, etc.)
- The writing style has strong reader appeal; it will hold readers' interest.
- The subject matter of the book has strong reader appeal.
- The book has "freshness;" it is not trite in its approach, plot, or style.
- The book is credible; its plot, approach or advice is reasonable and believable.

---

* Quantities, percents, and periods of time will vary with each publisher's scheduling, pricing, size of staff, market, advertising, etc.

- The manuscript will be well prepared, presented on computer disk with accompanying hard copy, with photo locations properly marked, photos properly captioned, pages numbered in order, etc. so minimal author contacts requesting manuscript quality improvements will be required.

15. Author Stature and Participation

- The author is a well-known individual with substantial readership appeal.
- The author is suitably qualified to write on the specified subject.
- The author will function compatibly with the company.
- The author has potential for writing future books for the company.
- The author will purchase significant quantities of the book for personal use and resale.
- The author can and will participate effectively in sales and marketing activities to promote the book.

16. Production Timing

- The manuscript will be available in time for normal production prior to the scheduled release date.

17. Book Format

- The book can be produced in standard formats which are generally accepted within the industry and which will fit vendor shelves, racks, etc.
- The author is in agreement with the company as to the book's published format (size, hardcover or paperbound, etc.).
- Photos, drawings, and charts of good quality have been supplied by the author, if appropriate.
- Strong cover art or a strong cover photo is available.

18. Book Length

- The book will be within suitable length parameters for its market.
- The book is of appropriate length that it can be priced at full price per page, rather than discounting it because of excess length.

19. Editorial Plan Compatibility

- The book correlates effectively with the company's long-range editorial plan for new releases.

20. Other Product Relationships

- The book will not have a negative impact on, nor reduce sales of any other company product.
- The book can be promoted and marketed in conjunction with other company products.

5

A Subject-Matter Analysis of Best-Selling Trade Books

INTRODUCTION

What sells? The answer to this often-asked question varies from year to year, and from decade to decade. It's influenced by world happenings and current events. It's shaped by new discoveries, new ways of doing things, new educational approaches, new technologies. It's influenced by fluctuating social standards, religious beliefs, community and national aspirations. The rise and fall of famous leaders, noted educators, profound thinkers and philosophers, great artists and composers, talented performers and other celebrities, and other charismatic personalities all shape the marketplace. Great natural disasters, wars, social turmoils, changes in modes of transportation, business methodologies, shifts in fashions and apparel—all these things influence what sells in the book industry.

But answering the question "what sells?" is an essential task for every author. He or she must decide what to write about. He must conceive the "compelling unique features" that will attract potential readers to the work he wants to write.

Just like individuals entering the world of work ultimately have to choose a profession or line of work, authors have to select the genre of writing they plan to pursue. Until they have made that selection, they usually can't begin to write successfully or distinguish themselves in a specific subject area.

Provided in this chapter is a publishing history that tracks major book sales in fourteen categories: seven fiction and seven non-fiction. The names of many authors and book titles are mentioned to help define the various subject categories.

For what purposes? To help authors (1) identify the subject areas in which they have the greatest desire to write, (2) identify successful authors in the various subject categories—individuals they can select as potential mentors and tutors, (3) identify books they may choose to read as writing models—books from which they can draw writing techniques, formats and plot formulas, and (4) provide popularity rankings and percentages which can assist authors in evaluating and determining the comparative overall level of readers' interest and category stability over an extended period of publishing history.

DESCRIPTION OF THE LISTS

During the period when the following data were gathered, *Publishers Weekly* magazine, which circulates on a weekly basis, published four separate lists which were compiled into a single list for analysis purposes in this study. The four lists are:

1. *Hardcover Fiction Best-sellers* (15 books),
2. *Hardcover Non-fiction Best-sellers* (15 books),
3. *Mass Market Paperback Best-sellers* (15 books), and
4. *Trade Paperback Best-sellers* (10 books).

An issue from each month, beginning with July, 1983, was selected for analysis. Usually the list from the first issue-week of the month was utilized. Consecutive weekly issues were never used, in order to nullify the effect of the occasional rapid entry and exit of various titles from the best-seller listings.

A judgment often had to be made as to which category to place a book, but once a category was assigned the book remained in it. When a hardcover book was reissued as a paperback it was left in the original category. No effort was made to separate the hardcover and paperback books in each category.

Though the formal category analysis depicted in the chart on page 96 ends in 1993, the commentary reflects best-sellers through mid-1998.

THE SUBJECT CATEGORIES

The purpose of the analysis was to determine the relative popularity of various book subject categories.

The seven fiction categories are listed and identified as follows:

1. ***Fiction: Adventure***—*fast-paced action novels, including spy and espionage thrillers.* Authors whose works appear regularly in this category are Tom Clancy, Jeffery Archer, James Clavell, Ken Follett, Robert Ludlum, Lawrence Saunders, Stephen Coonts, Jack Higgins, and Len Deighton. In the past five years, the number of books making the best sellers in this category have fallen off, perhaps because of the

demise of the communistic States. Tom Clancy continues to be successful with his novels such as *The Op Center.*

2. ***Fiction: Biographical and/or Historical***—*novels based on actual people and well-known historical events.* Typical subjects and authors are the U.S. historical novels of John Jakes; the "state" books of Dana Fuller Ross; James Michener's *Legacy, Texas, Alaska* and *Mexico;* Gore Vidal's *Lincoln*; Edward Rutherfurd's *Sarum*; and the 50th anniversary issue of *Gone With the Wind.* James Clavell's books, the war novels of W.E.B. Griffin, and the controversial *The Satanic Verses* have been placed in this category. *Schindler's List* and *The English Patient* did well with their movie tie-ins. Wilbur Smith enjoyed success with *River God* about Egypt. A small book, *Mutant Messages,* about a woman's walk-about in Australia with aborigines, did well for about a year and is still used in some college classes for its message about ecology. *Primary Colors,* based on the primary election of Bill Clinton, hit the charts in early 1996. Recent events in President Clinton's life and a movie of the same name has renewed interest in this book.

3. ***Fiction: General***—*novels of broad general interest which don't fit into the other fiction categories,* such as Pat Coroy's *Prince of Tides,* Ernest Hemingway's *The Garden of Eden,* Tom Wolfe's *The Bonfire of the Vanities,* Anne Tyler's *The Accidental Tourist, Love in the Time of Cholera, The Cider House Rules,* and the *Lake Woebegon* books by Garrison Keillor. Larry McMurty's books are included in this category except *The Lonesome Dove,* which is classified as a Western. *The Celestine Prophecy* by James Redford, which is supposedly a copy of an ancient manuscript found in Peru giving the secrets of a fulfilled life, has had phenomenal success on the charts for the past four years.

4. ***Fiction: Crime, Mystery and Horror***—*novels based on mystery, detective and police stories and those emphasizing shock and horror themes.* Typical authors are Steven King (with several titles appearing at the same time), Dean Koontz, Dick Francis, Robin Cook, and Martha Grimes.

Other representative books are Scott Turow's *Presumed Innocent*, *The 2 Mrs. Grenvilles*, *The Cat Who Walks Through Walls*, and the *Mission Earth* series. This category has enjoyed the largest growth in the past five years. Often half the best-seller fiction listings in any given week will be from this category. The novels of Steven King and Dean Koontz appear on the lists before their release date because of pre-publication sales, and their newer books seem to be written for even greater shock value. Robin Cook, Lillian Jackson and Sue Grafton continue with their successful series. The most famous and widely-read recent author is John Grisham with his lawyer-based stories *A Time to Kill, The Firm, The Pelican Brief, The Client, The Chamber, The Rainmaker, The Runaway Jury*, *The Partner,* and *The Street Lawyer*. Patricia Cornwall's Kay Scarpetta, as a Medical Examiner, is very popular with *Postmortem, Body of Evidence, All That Remains, Cruel & Unusual*, and *Body Farm*. Michael Palmer writes the medical thrillers *The Sisterhood, Side Effects, Flashback, Extreme Measures, Natural Causes, Silent Treatment* and *Critical Judgment*. Michael Crichton's *Jurassic Park, The Lost World,* and *Disclosure* helped revive his older books *Congo, Andromeda Strain, Sphere,* and *Rising Sun*. The gentler mysteries of Mary Higgins Clark, *Where Are the Children? The Cradle Will Fall,* and *A Stranger Is Watching* have also increased in sales with the success of her newer titles such as *I'll Be Seeing You, Loves Music, Loves to Dance, Remember Me, Let Me Call You Sweetheart* and *The Lottery Winner*.

5. ***Fiction: Romance and Women's***—*novels written specifically for a feminine audience using the typical "romance" formula, often with "victorian" plots*. Some authors seem to fall more clearly into this category than any other. Typical authors are Danielle Steel (many months with several titles all listed simultaneously), Margaret Atwood, Jude Deveraux, V. C. Andrews, Jean Auel, Barbara Taylor Bradford, Victoria Holt, Judith Krantz, Helen MacInnes, and Sidney Sheldon. This category shows the second strongest percentage in recent years. Belva Plain, Catherine Coulter,

LaVyrle Spencer and Danielle Steel keep writing successful novels. New writers have appeared: Laura Esquivel, *Like Water for Chocolate;* Amy Tan, *Joy Luck Club* and Robert James Waller, *The Bridges of Madison County.*

6. ***Fiction: Science Fiction and Fantasy****—novels with fanciful and futuristic plots.* Authors are more diversified here but the more popular ones are Isaac Asimov, Ron Huber, Anne McCaffrey, and Carl Sagan. The *Dune* and *Twins* series also have been prominent. The interest in space travel and spin-offs from movies and television shows about space such as *Star Wars* and *Star Trek* have kept this category alive, but books come and go off the lists quite quickly.

7. ***Fiction: Western****—novels based in the western territories of the United States during the last two centuries.* Except for two titles, all the books were written by Louis L'Amour. After his death, few books have appeared in this category. Larry McMurty has written several western novels such as the *Streets of Laredo* and Nicholas Evans' *Horse Whisperers* have kept this category alive, but it has the fewest books appearing on the fiction best-sellers lists.

The seven non-fiction categories include:

8. ***Biography****—books written by or about well-known individuals of the present.* These include political figures, businessmen, sports figures and movie stars. Many are written or ghost written by the individuals themselves. However, the "unauthorized biography" will often hit the best-seller list. Titles include *Iococca, Yeager, Intellectuals, Life and Death in Shanghai* and *West with the Night.* Other subjects are Gracie Burns, Peter Lynch, Donald Trump, Frank Sinatra, Marilyn Monroe, Rock Hudson, Shirley MacLaine (with several titles), Louis L'Amour, Jim McMahon and Picasso. The writings of James Herriot and Isak Dinesen are included in this category. America's interest in people-watching has increased the readership in this category. O.J. Simpson, several lawyers and Mark Fuhrman, the police officer, all wrote quick best-seller books about the trials. At the time of Princess Diana's death there were at least four books about her on the list in any

given week for several months. The most recent list, at the time of going to press with this book, features four books on the *Titantic* disaster and three more about Leonardo Dicaprio (a star of the movie), comprising seven of the 15 non-fiction best sellers for that week. Biographies about individual people such as *Having Our Say* (two black sisters) and *The Color of Water* (a black man raised by a white mother) and the poetry by Maya Angelou *I Know Why the Caged Bird Sings,* reflect awareness of African-Americans' contribution to literature.

9. ***Business and Finance****—books on the popular aspects of business, financial advice, money management, income tax helps* (a seasonal addition to the lists), *and legal questions.* This category was much more active the first three years of the study because of two of the most popular books of the study: *The One-minute Manager* (appearing for 33 months) and *In Search of Excellence* (32 months). Other titles included *Megatrends, What They Don't Teach You at Harvard Business School, What Color is Your Parachute?, Swim with the Sharks Without Being Eaten Alive,* and *Leadership Secrets of Attila the Hun.* Stephen Covey's *The 7 Habits of Highly Effective People, The 7 Habits of Highly Effective Families* and *First Things First* are the recent leaders in this category for the past three years.

10. ***History, Current Events and Reference****—books dealing with world events, U.S. government, and basic subjects which affect the general populace.* Titles include *A Day in the Life of America, The Good War, Adult Children of Alcoholics, A Brief History of Time, Rise and Fall of the Great Powers, A Season on the Brink,* and several books on AIDS. *Undaunted Courage,* about Thomas Jefferson, and *We Were Soldiers Once,* about Viet Nam, and *Zlate's Diary,* from a young girl in Sarejavo reflect interest in various historical periods. Also included in this category are books written about actual criminal events such as *Midnight in the Garden of Good and Evil,* which has been on the lists for the past four years. Reference books such as *Webster's New Ninth Collegiate Dictionary, The Farmer's Almanac, The Book of*

Questions, and *The Way Things Work* also are in this category.

11. ***Diet, Beauty and Fitness***—*books on general health and nutrition, beauty advice, specific diets, and recipe books.* Also in this category are titles on *physical fitness, personal conditioning and exercise workout books.* This category has seen a slow decline in the best-seller listings during this study. Titles include *The 8-Week Cholesterol Cure, The Frugal Gourmet* books, *Fit for Life, Callanetics, The Rotation Diets* and *Color Me Beautiful.* The rewrite of *Dr. Atkins' Diet* and the publication of books on the *T-Factor Fat Gram* and *The Zone* diet has increased sales in this category.

12. ***How-to and Lifestyle***—*advice on the aspects of personal improvement and instructions on the performance of a specific skill or procedure.* Authors include Leo Buscaglia and Robert Schuller. Additional titles are *The Road Less Traveled* (the most popular book of the study, on the list for over ten years), *Dianetics, Codependent No More, Women Who Love Too Much, Smart Women, Foolish Choices*, and *All I Really Need to Know I Learned in Kindergarten.* This category has had the highest percentage of best-sellers in the non-fiction lists. People are searching for ways to better themselves and their relationships with others. Recent titles include *Care of the Soul, Silent Passage, Love Medicine and Miracles, Soulmates, Simple Abundance, Sisters, Stupid Things Men Do to Mess Up Their Lives, Reviving Ophelia* and the most popular *Men are From Mars, Women Are From Venus* and its spinoffs by John Gray. Another subject area in this category is "feel-good" books like *Don't Sweat the Small Stuff . . . and It's All Small Stuff,* by Richard Carlson, *The Book of Virtues* by William Bennett, *It Takes a Village* by Hillary Rodham Clinton, and *The Chicken Soup for the Soul* series have been very popular. One of the newest phenomena is the books on near-death experiences and the existence of angels: *Embraced By the Light, Saved by the Light, How We Die*, and *Where Angels Walk.*

13. ***Humor***—*humorous essays and cartoon collections.* Included are Bill Cosby's *Fatherhood, Time Flies*, and *Love*

and Marriage; Erma Bombeck's *Motherhood, the Second Oldest Profession* and *Family: The Ties That Bind . . .* and *Gag!;* Dr. Seuss's *You're Only Old Once;* and books by humorist Art Buchwald, Andy Rooney, Dave Barry and Rush Limbaugh. Actor Paul Reiser's books on *Couplehood* and *Babyhood* and Tim Allen's *Don't Stand Too Close to the Naked Man* add to this category. Cartoonists (many times with more than one book on the list) include Gary Larson's *Far Side* series, Bill Watterson's *Calvin and Hobbes* series, Jim Davis's *Garfield* books and the *Berke Breatheds* books.

14. ***Travel****—includes road atlases and commentaries on tourist attractions.* Every summer the *Road Atlas* appears. Other titles in this smallest category are *Across China, On the Road with Charles Kuralt,* and *The Year In Provence* and *Toujorce Provence* by Peter Mayle.

ANALYSIS OF THE DATA

The 55 best-selling titles were analyzed and classified as to subject matter since July 1983. The following is a summary of the analysis conclusions, through 1993.

1. Fiction is slightly more popular than nonfiction, with 2,090 of the 3,905 total books' listings falling into the fiction category (53.52%).

2. Many authors' works achieve best-seller status on the basis of the author's reputation alone—often during pre-publication sales.

3. Ranked by subject matter in descending order, the most popular subjects among trade books are:

1	Fiction: Romance and Women's	15.11%
2	Fiction: Adventure	10.42%
3	How-to and Lifestyle	10.14%
4	Biography	10.01%
5	Fiction: Mystery and Horror	9.32%
6	History, Current Events and Reference	7.40%
7	Humor	6.48%
8	Fiction: Biographical and Historical	6.20%
9	Fiction: Science Fiction and Fantasy	5.81%

10 Diet, Beauty and Fitness 5.69%
11 Business and Finance 5.66%
12 Fiction: General. 5.12%
13 Fiction: Western 1.54%
14 Travel 10%

4. An analysis of the listings each year show that there is an ebb and flow of the popularity of the various subject categories.

Subject-Matter Analysis of Best-Selling Books in the General Book Market Compiled from Books Listed in *Publishers' Weekly* Magazine

	1983 %	1984 %	1985 %	1986 %	1987 %	1988 %	1989 %	1990 %	1991 %	1992 %	1993 %	11-Yr Avg %
Fiction:												
Romance & Women's Stories	15.2	14.7	17.0	15.8	12.9	14.4	17.9	16.4	17.9	17.0	8.9	**15.3**
Horror & Mystery	15.2	7.4	8.3	7.9	9.7	10.2	8.6	11.4	14.4	15.2	20.0	**11.6**
Adventure & Espionage	7.6	10.6	11.2	10.9	12.1	8.5	11.7	10.3	6.8	8.0	4.5	**9.3**
General	1.5	3.5	3.9	5.2	3.8	8.9	9.2	7.6	7.0	8.6	9.4	**6.2**
Biographical, Historical	7.0	8.3	6.5	7.4	4.7	4.8	4.6	2.4	3.0	2.1	5.0	**5.1**
Science Fiction & Fantasy	8.5	7.7	6.1	5.2	5.2	5.5	1.9	2.3	3.2	2.9	2.8	**4.7**
Western	0.9	1.1	2.3	2.7	1.4	0.6	1.1	1.4	1.7	0.3	0.0	**1.2**
Total Fiction Percentages	**56.0**	**53.0**	**55.0**	**55.0**	**50.0**	**53.0**	**55.3**	**51.5**	**53.9**	**54.0**	**50.5**	**53.4**
Non-Fiction:												
How-to & Lifestyle	8.5	10.6	9.7	11.4	10.6	9.7	11.0	11.7	12.9	13.3	17.8	**11.6**
Biography	6.4	7.3	10.0	10.0	11.5	13.3	10.6	12.9	10.3	11.8	15.0	**10.8**
History, Current Events, Reference	2.7	7.1	3.5	4.2	10.5	11.4	10.5	8.8	7.6	7.1	8.9	**7.5**
Business & Finance	10.6	10.2	8.9	4.1	1.5	1.7	3.5	7.1	6.2	4.2	4.5	**5.7**
Humor	7.0	5.6	4.5	6.7	8.5	7.0	5.3	4.7	5.2	6.1	1.1	**5.6**
Diet, Beauty & Fitness	8.5	5.5	6.8	6.8	5.6	3.6	3.8	3.0	2.1	2.3	2.2	**4.6**
Travel	0.9	0.5	1.2	1.8	2.1	0.5	0.2	0.5	1.8	1.2	0.0	**1.0**
Total Non-Fiction Percentages	**44.0**	**47.0**	**45.0**	**45.0**	**50.0**	**47.0**	**44.7**	**48.5**	**46.1**	**46.0**	**49.5**	**46.6**
Combined Total	100.0	100.0	100.0	100.0	100.0	100.0	100.0	100.0	100.0	100.0	100.0	**100.0**

6

A Subject-Matter Analysis of Best-Selling Religious Books

INTRODUCTION

Writing for the religious marketplace is a unique and challenging endeavor. If your goal as an author is to lift and inspire, to instruct others in religiously oriented patterns for happy and successful living, to analyze and glean meanings from sacred scriptures, or to proselyte, indoctrinate, win converts for and defend a particular religion or set of religious dogmas, this is the area for you.

In this chapter, the religious best-sellers of the past decade-and-a-half are classified into eleven broad categories. Each category is carefully defined, with the names of prominent authors and book titles listed.

Several categories can be combined into even larger groupings. Thus the three categories *Personal Development and Christian Life, Inspirational,* and *Marriage and Family Life* are linked together as the "***social gospel***," comprising 60.49% of the total religious-book sales. The three categories of *Doctrinal, Scriptural* and *Eschatalogical* can be combined into an overall category of "***doctrinal and scriptural studies***" which in the aggregate account for 9.87% of total religious-book sales.

Pages 101-02 draw significant observations on how the trade and religious marketplaces differ, and how authors vary their approach as they write for them.

Again, this chapter, like the chapter which precedes it, is written to assist authors and publishers in determining potential new areas for further writing and publishing—in effect it is written to help them discover their niche.

DESCRIPTION OF THE LISTS

Bookstore Journal Magazine, a trade journal published for the Christian Booksellers Association, publishes best-seller lists of books produced for the Christian market. For years they have published lists of the ten best-selling clothbound and ten best-selling paperback Christian books. These twenty titles have been analyzed for subject-matter content on a monthly basis since July, 1983.

In March of 1989 the listing was changed to combine the CBA services and the *Spring Arbor Distributors' List*. At that time the lists were expanded to 20 titles in each of the clothbound and paperback lists. Since this statistical study was begun with 10 titles from each group, we continued to report on the top 10 of each list.

THE SUBJECT CATEGORIES

The purpose of the study was to determine the relative popularity of various book subject categories. As the study began, it was found that the books typically fell into eleven different categories. A decision sometimes had to be made concerning in which category a book should be placed. However, once a book was placed in a category it remained there, even though it might later be reissued as a paperback.

The categories were selected as follows:

1. ***Doctrinal****—books written about an identifiable Christian doctrine or group of related doctrines.* Titles include C.S. Lewis's *Mere Christianity* (which has appeared and reappeared consistently throughout the study), Pat Robertson's *Answers to 200 of Life's Most Probing Questions*, and Dave Hunt's *The Seduction of Christianity* and *Beyond Seduction.*

2. ***Scriptural****—books based on a specific area of the Bible,* such as *A Shepherd Looks at Psalm 23* and *The Gospel According to Jesus.*

3. ***Eschatological****—books about prophecy and future "last days" events* such as Hal Lindsey's books, Billy Graham's *Approaching Hoofbeats of the Four Horsemen of the Apocalypse* and books such as *Peace, Prosperity & the Coming Holocaust* and *88 Reasons Why the Rapture is in 1988.*

4. ***Inspirational****—books written to inspire the reader to believe with faith in a better life,* often scripturally based. Titles include Pat Robertson's *Secret Kingdom,* Jerry Bridges' *Pursuit of Holiness,* Billy Graham's *Unto The Hills,* and titles by Charles Colson. Other popular titles were *My Utmost for His Highest, The Road Unseen, Hind's Feet on High Places,* and *Rekindled.*

5. ***Biographical****—books about a specific (usually living) person, including his personal history and philosophy of life.* Examples include *Choices—Changes* by Joni Eareckson Tada, *Angels Watching over Me,* by Betty Malz, *I Gave God Time,* by Ann Kimel Anderson, *Ashes to Gold,* by Patti Roberts, *David,* by Mane Rothenberg, and *Plain Bread* by Ben Kinchlow.

6. ***Personal Development and Christian Life****—books on improving one's personality or lifestyle, written from a "believing" viewpoint.* Charles Swindoll has been the most prolific author of this category, sometimes with multiple books listed during the same month such as *Strengthening Your Grip, Improving Your Serve, Growing Strong in the Seasons of Life,* and *Living Above the Level of Mediocrity.* Robert Schuller's *Tough Times Never Last But Tough People Do,* and *The Blessing* by Smalley and Trent, have been strong on the lists. Other popular titles include *Inside Out, Good Grief, Free to Be Thin, Seeds of Greatness, Ordering Your Private World* and *Healing for Damaged Emotions.*

7. ***Marriage and Family Life****—books encouraging the development of a Christian home, instructions on how to raise children and developing strong personal and marriage relationships.* James Dobson is the most popular author with *Love for a Lifetime, Love Must Be Tough, Dare to Discipline,* and *The Strong-willed Child,* often on the lists at the same time. Other titles are *Growing Wise in Family Life, Love Life for Every Married Couple, Parents and Teenagers, Raising Positive Kids in a Negative World,* Tim LaHaye's *Act of Marriage,* and Joyce Landorf's *He Began With Eve.*

8. ***Current Religious Events and Issues****—religious and theological sects of current interest or notoriety.* These subjects include books on the "New Age," especially those by Texe Manes, *20 Hot Potatoes Christians Are Afraid to Touch, Child*

Abuse in the Classroom, Hidden Dangers of the Rainbow, Exodus II, and Ronald Reagan's *Abortion and the Conscience of a Nation.*

9. ***Religious Fiction****—novels with a religious slant* such as *Winter is Not Forever, Love Takes Wing, This Present Darkness, When Calls the Heart,* and *Love's Abiding Joy.* Janet Oke is the most prolific author in this category.

10. ***Youth Books****—personality and youth guidance books directed especially towards teenagers.* James Dobson's *Preparing for Adolescence* has been the most popular title in this category.

11. ***Children's Books****—materials for children under twelve years of age.* This is the smallest category of the study, with Kenneth Taylor's *Bible in Pictures for Little Eyes* being the most common title. Only seven months had a children's title listed. In May 1989, *Bookstore Journal* began a separate 20-title listing of best-selling Christian Children's Books. This category was dropped from the analysis from that month forward.

ANALYSIS OF THE DATA

An analysis of the data gathered shows the following:

1. Three themes dominate the market, with 1,015 books, or 60.49 % of the best-sellers, in the categories of *Personal Development and Christian Life, Inspirational,* and *Marriage and Family Life.* In bookstore terms, these books preach the "social gospel."

2. Doctrinal and scriptural studies rank low in the listings. Only 139 of the 1,440 total books fall into the categories of *Doctrinal, Scriptural,* and *Eschatalogical.* This may be because these types of books usually have a strong denominational perspective, which prevents them from attaining national best-seller status.

3. Four strong differences can be noted between the General and Christian best-seller markets:

First: The books on the Christian lists tend to remain on lists much longer (some over five years, becoming "classics"). They also drop off and reappear back on the lists more often.

Second: Authors in the General market tend to write only one type of book. But in the Christian market, diversified books by the same author appear in different categories, often during the same month.

Third: The total number of copies needed to make a best-seller in the Christian market is generally much lower than those in the General market. However, a popular cloth-bound book follows the same procedure of being reissued as a paperback.

Fourth: In the general marketplace, fiction is slightly more popular than non-fiction, garnering 53.52% of the best-seller rankings. But in the Christian marketplace, fiction ranks fourth, comprising only 6.97% of the best-sellers listed. The three non-fiction categories ahead of religious fiction, with 70.46% of the titles, are *Personal Development and Christian Life, Inspirational,* and *Marriage and Family Life.*

4. Ranked by subject matter in descending order, the cumulative category popularity ranking in the Christian Booksellers marketplace is as follows:

1	Personal Development and Christian Life	29.61%
2	Inspirational	21.71%
3	Marriage and Family Life	19.14%
4	Religious Fiction	6.97%
5	Current Religious Events and Issues	5.99%
6	Doctrinal	5.33%
7	Biographical	3.55%
8	Eschatalogical	2.63%
9	Books for Youth	2.70%
10	Scriptural	1.91%
11	Children's Books	.46%

5. An analysis of the listings for each year clearly shows that there is an increase and decrease of the popularity of various subjects. To follow these trends, a percentage has been calculated yearly for each category, as is shown on the following page.

Subject-Matter Analysis of Best-Selling Books in the General Christian Bookstore Market Compiled from Lists Published in the *Bookstore Journal* Magazine

	1983 %	1984 %	1985 %	1986 %	1987 %	1988 %	1989 %	1990 %	1991 %	1992 %	1993 %	11-Yr Avg %
Inspirational	18.4	25.0	28.9	25.8	16.3	17.9	19.6	26.0	26.9	26.9	35.6	**24.3**
Personal Development & Christian Life	25.9	27.1	32.8	30.8	33.8	26.7	22.7	12.7	16.3	15.8	13.1	**23.4**
Marriage & Family Life	20.2	17.5	19.6	16.3	16.3	24.2	23.4	20.4	16.9	15.0	13.1	**18.4**
Religious Fiction	5.9	4.2	2.9	7.1	7.5	8.3	14.8	20.4	22.5	24.4	25.0	**13.0**
Current Religious Events & Issues	2.6	10.8	3.3	2.1	4.6	11.3	4.8	4.6	7.7	11.3	6.9	**6.4**
Doctrinal	1.7	3.8	4.9	8.2	11.3	2.9	2.7	2.3	1.9	1.9	1.3	**3.9**
Biographical	5.9	2.5	4.5	5.9	5.0	0.4	2.7	5.4	3.5	1.9	2.5	**3.7**
Scriptural	4.3	0.0	0.0	0.0	0.8	2.1	8.0	6.5	1.9	2.9	0.6	**2.5**
Eschatalogical	10.1	7.9	0.4	2.1	0.4	0.8	0.2	0.0	1.5	0.0	1.9	**2.3**
Books for Youth	2.5	0.8	1.5	1.7	4.2	5.4	1.1	1.7	1.0	0.0	0.0	**1.8**
*Children's Books**	2.5	0.4	1.1	0.0	0.0	0.0	0.0	0.0	0.0	0.0	0.0	**0.4**
Total Percentages	100.0	100.0	100.0	100.0	100.0	100.0	100.0	100.0	100.0	100.0	100.0	**100.0**

* This category was discontinued in 1989.

7

Basic Book Publishing Industry Practices: Sales and Printing

INTRODUCTION

How many copies are sold of an average hardbound book today? How long will it remain in print, and when will most of its sales occur? How many books must be sold for a typical hardcover book to be a best-seller? These are typical of questions asked of major book publishers in two surveys taken by the author at the 1987 and 1988 American Booksellers Association national conventions.

The surveys focused on the average hardbound book that makes up the majority of offerings from book publishers today. They eliminated the skewing of data caused by the few books which receive special treatment because they've been picked for "bestseller" treatment.

Prepared by a publishing professional as part of an M.B.A. degree thesis, the data gathered presents a valuable overview of basic approaches currently utilized in the book publishing industry.

The surveys' results reflected insights which were difficult to obtain within the industry, providing valuable "ball park" answers to questions concerning procedures and practices which were not readily available in written form within the trade. They also provided a glimpse of the practices and policies of some of the largest and most renowned publishing firms in the nation.

HOW THE SURVEYS WERE TAKEN

The procedure used at the conventions was to approach representatives of various firms and indicate that a survey was being taken to complete an M.B.A. case project. The one-page survey form was then shown to the publisher's representative, and almost invariably that person would call for the company's advertising, marketing, or promotion manager who would in turn fill out the questionnaire. Thirty-one well-known publishers were surveyed in this manner in

1987, and thirty were surveyed during the 1988 ABA convention.

An effort was made to strike a balance among the types of companies approached. In addition to big-name general publishers, major publishers in the Christian booksellers market were approached. Several large college presses were included in the surveys also. All firms contacted were medium and large publishing companies. Every company surveyed was a well-known business with high name recognition in the publishing arena. No small "one-man" or "family" publishers were included. All firms interviewed were situated in the main area of the exhibit hall rather than in the "small press" section, and were operating at least two convention booths at the national conventions.

Though the surveys provide valuable insights, they have weaknesses which should be noted. The information obtained was "off the cuff," delivered without benefit of exact records, budgets, written product histories and marketing plans. Also, in some instances, the information was not provided by the most knowledgeable individual in the companies surveyed, but rather by the person considered most qualified who happened to be in the booth as the survey approaches were made. But even with these limitations, the surveys present a valuable "consensus" overview of some essential aspects and "rules of thumb" of the book publishing industry based on the practices and opinions of professionals in the field.

They have added significance because they compile data which typically is regarded as confidential by many firms, combining that data to give a significant industry-wide picture of day-to-day results and expectations concerning typical, "non-hyped" book offerings.

TYPICAL FIRST-EDITION PRINT QUANTITY

Insights were gained concerning the initial quantity of books printed for a hardcover book. The question was asked, "*What is your company's usual first printing quantity of a typical hardbound book which you estimate will be an average seller?"*

The ***mean*** of their combined answers to this question was ***12,027 books.*** The median was 10,000, situated in a range from a minimum of 3,000 books to a maximum of 30,000 books.

QUANTITY OF BOOKS PRESOLD

It appears that major publishers expend considerable effort to presell their books before they come off the press. The question was asked, "*What quantity of a typical hardbound book does your company attempt to have presold before the book is first printed?*"

Analysis of the results showed that a ***mean*** percentage of ***59.17%*** of hardbound books are presold before the first edition goes to press. Responses to this question had a wide range, from 16.7% up to 100%. The distribution was relatively even throughout the range.

AVERAGE MONTHS A BOOK REMAINS IN PRINT

Another question on the surveys asked, "*How many months does an average-selling book typically remain in print?*"

An analysis of the responses showed the mean number of months a book remains in print was ***43.07 months***. The range was wide on this question, however, with answers ranging from 120 months (10 years) down to 12 months (1 year).

Several answers pertaining to this question were eliminated from the study because they represented the treatment of "classics," or textbooks, or items such as almanacs which are periodically updated but never allowed to go permanently out of print. Several answers pertaining to these types of materials fell into the 35- to 50-year range. Those special items were identified and noted as the survey was taken.

The answers to this question were *heavily skewed to the low end*, with 17.9% reporting a book's life expectancy to be only between 21.8 and 31.6 months, and 39.3% indicating a book's life expectancy to be between 31.6 and 41.4 months, so almost 50% of the responses indicated the typical book for that publisher would be out of print in three years or less.

QUARTERLY SALES OF NEW BOOKS

The question was asked, "*What percent of sales would your company expect to occur in each quarter of the life cycle of a typical hardcover book?*" Spaces were then provided to write a percentage figure for each of ten quarters. The mean percents for the first four quarters were as follows:

CUMULATIVE SALES PER QUARTER
During a Book's First Year

Quarter	% of Sales in Quarter	Cumulative % of Sales
1	43.25	43.25
2	20.25	63.50
3	14.38	77.88
4	13.26	91.14

Sales during the remaining six quarters were so negligible that they were not compiled. It is obvious from the survey that *most books are seen as having a product life cycle that is almost complete within the first year.* If the typical book remains in print for 43 months, as is indicated above, that leaves only 8.86% of the book's sales to be divided over the final 31 months of the book's life.

PRODUCT LIFE CYCLE EXPECTATIONS
Phase Length and Percent of Total Sales

These figures, taken from the first year's survey, aid in defining a book's life cycle. Assuming the above figures to be typical, the product life cycle for a typical book might be defined as approximately:

Stage	**Length**
Introductory Stage	2 months
Growth Stage	6 months
Maturity Stage	6 months
Decline Stage	29 months
Total book life:	43 months

There was considerable variation in the percent of sales reported for each of the first four quarters.

Quarter one, with a ***mean*** of ***43.25%***, ranged from a minimum of 10% to a maximum of 85%. There was a fairly balanced spread throughout the range, but with 26.7% of the replies arrayed between 23.5% and 30.4% of total sales occurring during the first quarter. Another 26.7% of the replies indicated the expectation that between 44.1 and 50.9% of total sales would take place during the first quarter.

Quarter two, with a ***mean*** of ***20.25%*** of total book sales expected, had a range from 10% minimum to 75% maximum. This quarter was highly skewed, with 8% of those surveyed reporting sales expectations for the quarter at the low end of the book's total sales, between 10% and 21.8%.

Quarter three, with a ***mean*** of ***14.38%*** of total book sales expected, and quarter four, with a mean of 13.26%, were very similar. Both had ranges from 4 to 50%; both were strongly skewed to the low end.

Quarter four showed **76%** of the responses between 4% and 12.36%.

MONTHS IN A BOOK'S INTRODUCTORY AND GROWTH PHASES

This subject was explored in greater depth during the second survey. The publishers were asked, "*For an average book's product life cycle, how many months are in its (A) Introductory Phase, and (B) Growth Phase?*"

The expressed range for a new book's ***Introductory Phase*** was broad, extending from "three weeks" to "six months." This reflects the many different types of books introduced into the marketplace and the varying approaches used to introduce them. The average of all the replies received was 81.1 days (about 2.7 months). However, two particularly long estimates seemed to skew the data unrealistically. With those long estimates removed, the mean length of a book's introductory period shrank to ***65.7 days*** (about 2.2 months).

The expressed range for a typical book's ***Growth Phase*** extended from "two months" to "one-and-a-half years," yielding an average of 205 days (about 6.8 months). But removing the same two long estimates reduced the *average to **150 days*** (about 5 months), which is much more in line with the figures gathered in the previous year's survey.

PERCENTAGES OF AN AVERAGE BOOK'S TOTAL SALES IN ITS INTRODUCTORY AND GROWTH PHASES

To confirm data received in the first year's survey, a question in the second survey asked, "*What percent of the average book's total sales occur in its (A) introductory phase, and (B) its growth phase?*" Expressed percentages of a book's total sales for the ***Introductory Phase*** ranged from 17% to 60%, with the ***mean*** coming out to ***34.3%***. Again, two extremely high answers of 60% of sales occurring in the introductory phase appeared to skew the data. With those two responses removed, the percentage of books sold during the book's *introductory phase averaged out to **28.6%.***

Responses from the second survey pertaining to the percentage of books sold during the book's ***Growth Phase*** ranged from 20 to 50 percent. The ***mean*** answer was ***37.3%***. Removing the two 20% answers which were perceived to be abnormally low because 60% of sales were attributed to the book's introductory period lifted the *mean **Growth Phase Sales** to **41.1%*** of the book's total sales, a more realistic figure for a typical growth phase in the book industry.

SALES REQUIRED TO REACH BREAK-EVEN

Another question dealt with the number of book sales needed to reach essential publishing target levels. A question on the first survey inquired, "*How many copies of a typical hardbound book need to be sold for the book to break even?*"

The survey respondents indicated *a mean of **6,215** copies* were needed to break even for their companies. This field ranged from a minimum of 1,500 to a maximum of 20,000. The *median was **4,250** copies.*

Survey comments contained the obvious notations that the break-even point is highly dependent upon author royalties and advances and upon promotional expenses.

SALES REQUIRED TO ACHIEVE AVERAGE SALES

Survey participants were asked, "*How many total copies of an average-selling hardbound book does your company expect to sell?*" The respondents collectively indicated that *the average-selling book would sell **12,646** copies.*

This mean was above the median of 10,000 copies. The range extended from a minimum of 3,000 copies up to a maximum of 35,000 copies sold.

SALES REQUIRED TO BE A BEST-SELLER

Another question posed was, "*How many copies of a book must be sold for your company to regard it as being a best-seller?*" The mean answer to this query was ***37,708*** books.

The median answer was somewhat lower: 32,500 books. The range was from a minimum of 10,000 books up to a maximum of 80,000 books.

SALES REQUIRED TO APPEAR ON MAJOR BEST-SELLER LISTS

One of the most challenging questions asked in the surveys was, "*What quantity of books must be sold to position a book on major national best-seller lists?*"

The *mean answer was **70,139** copies.* The median answer was higher in this case: 75,000 books. The range was from 15,000 up to 150,000 copies.

This question brought more guesswork than the surveys' other queries, since many of the individuals responding to the survey questionnaires personally had not been involved with a book which reached the best-seller lists. Several comments, however, were significant.

First, it was pointed out that the quantity of books needed to hit the best-seller lists varies greatly at different times of the year, with a lesser quantity needed during the slow summer months than during the fall and spring seasons when many new titles are being pushed into the stores.

Second, it was observed that since key stores furnish the data for the makeup of the lists, systematic selling to those stores can influence the list somewhat.

Third, it also was pointed out that the timing of sales to those stores was critical; there must be very large sales in a very short period of time, typically about a week, for books to join the ranks of the nation's best-seller lists.

Fourth, it was observed that many types of books are not even candidates for the lists. Many books in other markets outsell the best sellers shown on the lists but don't get named to the lists because they flow through channels which do not report sales to the list compilers.

MOST PROFITABLE RETAIL PRICES FOR HARDBACKS AND TRADE PAPERBACKS

Everyone probably has his own theory on what is the "best" retail price for a book in today's market—the list price which provides the greatest profit without meeting price resistance from many customers. In an effort to identify those prices which were best in the market at that time, the ***1988*** survey asked, "*What's the best-yielding retail price for (A) hardcover and (B) trade paperback books today?*"

Respondents furnished both an "ideal" price and a range for both types of books. The expressed hardcover price range extended from $4.95 to $24.95, with the low end averaging to $14.78 and the upper end averaging to $20.37. The most-frequently suggested *"best" single hardcover price was* ***$18.95***, with the average of all the suggested "best" hardcover-book prices *averaging to $17.05*.

The "best" trade paperback ranges suggested had a low of $3.95 and a high of $15.95, with the low end of the range averaging to $7.55 and the upper end averaging to $12.55. The specific "best" prices suggested for trade paperbacks ranged from $7.95 to $12.95, with the average *"very best" price falling at* ***$10.15*** for a trade paperback book.

In summary, *average recommended prices of $17.05* for a hardback and *$10.15 recommended for a trade paperback* represented what the surveyed publishers felt would be the best prices for yielding good profitability without encountering sizeable price resistance from the buying public in 1988.

But a decade has gone by since the survey was taken, with annual inflation rates averaging around three percent, for a 10-year total inflation increase of 30%. Applying that percent of increase to the 1988 figures would make the **1998** "best" average suggested single hard-cover price ***$22.16***, and "very best" average suggested trade paperback price ***$13.19***.

8

Basic Book Publishing Industry Practices: Marketing

INTRODUCTION

What are the best months in which to release new books? How much money should be spent on pre-publication advertising, and how should these funds be allocated? What percent of a book's retail price should be spent on advertising? These are typical of the questions asked of major book publishers in two surveys taken by the author at the 1987 and 1988 American Booksellers Association national conventions.

The surveys focused on the average hardbound book that makes up the majority of offerings from book publishers today. They eliminated the skewing of data caused by the few books which receive special treatment because they've been picked for "bestseller" treatment.

Prepared by a publishing professional as part of an M.B.A. degree thesis, the data gathered present a valuable overview of basic approaches currently utilized in the book publishing industry.

The surveys' results reflected insights which were difficult to obtain within the industry and provided "ball park" answers to questions concerning procedures and practices which were not readily available in written form within the trade. They also provided a glimpse of the practices and policies of some of the largest and most renowned publishing firms in the nation.

HOW THE SURVEYS WERE TAKEN

The procedure used at the conventions was to approach representatives of various firms and indicate that a survey was being taken to complete an M.B.A. case project. The one-page survey form was then shown to the publisher's representative, and almost invariably that person would call for the company's advertising, marketing, or promotion manager who would in turn fill out the questionnaire. Thirty-one well-known publishers were surveyed in this manner in 1987, and thirty were surveyed during the 1988 ABA convention.

An effort was made to strike a balance among the types of companies approached. In addition to big-name general publishers, major publishers in the Christian booksellers market were approached. Several large college presses were included in the surveys also. All firms contacted were medium and large publishing companies. Every company surveyed was a well-known business with high name recognition in the publishing arena. No small "one-man" or "family" publishers were included. All firms interviewed were situated in the main area of the exhibit hall rather than in the "small press" section, and were operating at least two convention booths at the national convention.

Though the surveys provide valuable insights, they have weaknesses which should be noted. The information obtained was "off the cuff," delivered without benefit of exact records, budgets, written product histories and marketing plans. Also, in some instances the information was not provided by the most knowledgeable individual in the companies surveyed, but rather by the person considered most qualified who happened to be in the booth as the survey approaches were made. But even with these limitations, the surveys present a valuable "consensus" overview of some essential aspects and "rules of thumb" of the book publishing industry based on the practices and opinions of professionals in the field.

BEST MONTHS FOR NEW BOOK RELEASES

The survey's first questions were directed towards determining what months publishers consider best for releasing their new books. *The publishers were asked to identify the four months they believed to be the best for new releases, in preference order.* Their answers were then weighted, with first-choice months given 4 points, second-choice months given 3 points, etc.

The charted responses revealed some interesting insights, and show the relative strengths of fall versus spring release months:

Preferred Months For New Book Releases

Rank	Month	Percent
1	September	28.4%
2	August	16.4%
3	January	14.9%
4	October	12.7%
5	April	10.4%
6	February	5.2%
7	March	5.2%
8	June	3.0%
9	July	2.2%
10	May	1.6%
11	November	0.0%
12	December	0.0%

OPTIMAL INTERVAL BETWEEN A BOOK'S FIRST ANNOUNCEMENT AND PUBLICATION

The second query was aimed at determining how far in advance of actual release a book should be announced to potential buyers. Publishers were asked, "*What's the optimal time between the first announcement and actual release of a new book?*"

The answers spanned a range between "two months" and "six months," but the totals averaged out to ***111 days*** (about 3.67 months).

AMOUNT SPENT ON PRE-PUBLICATION ADVERTISING AND ITS ALLOCATION

The next two questions focused on what is typically done to announce "mid-list" books—titles which make up the heart of the new-book offerings for many publishers but which aren't their bestselling blockbusters. The question was asked, "*How much must be spent on pre-publication advertising to establish an average new book in the marketplace?*"

The responses proved to be surprisingly low. Several (including some of the very largest publishers) indicated that they spent nothing on pre-publication advertising for "average" books. The range for those who gave figures extended from a low of $875 up to a high of $6,250. The total range, when averaged, yielded a mean pre-publication expenditure of ***$3,302*** per title.

RELATIVE POPULARITY OF MEDIA FOR BOOK ANNOUNCEMENTS

It was obvious that the different publishers have varying approaches to pre-publication advertising, with funds for particular books specifically directed toward reaching the potential markets they have identified.

The relative popularity of various media as book announcement vehicles averaged out in this manner:

Announcement Media	Percent
Publishers Weekly	18%
American Bookseller	14%
Advance (Ingram)	14%
Book Alert or *Forecast* (Baker & Taylor)	14%
Library Journal	12%
Publisher's own catalog and literature	10%
Bound galleys, review copies mailings	8%
Other distributors' newsletters	4%
Religious trade publications (*Bookstore Journal, Christian Retailing*)	2%
Regional booksellers' catalogs	2%
Author promotions	2%
	100%

When asked "*How would your company actually allocate the funds you can use for pre-publication advertising?*" the publishers queried gave responses which averaged to the following:

ALLOCATION OF FUNDS FOR ANNOUNCEMENT MEDIA

Announcement Media	Percent
Publishers Weekly	27.6%
Library Journal	14.7%
American Bookseller	11.3%
Ingram	8.2%
Baker & Taylor	5.6%
Other expenditures	32.6%
	100.0%

The above data, of course, related to the pre-publication announcements of "average," or "mid-list" books. Time constraints prevented the surveying of what typical publishers would spend to introduce a book that was considered "better than average"—books for which considerable effort would be expended to establish them in the marketplace, but which were not targeted for all-out "bestseller" treatment.

A PUBLISHER'S PRE-PUBLICATION BOOK INTRODUCTION CAMPAIGN

One well-known publisher did outline a more advanced pre-publication book introduction campaign as follows:

Announcement Media	Expenditure	Percent
Convention Displays	$10,000	41.2%
Publishers Weekly ads	3,000	12.3%
Review copies, bound galleys mailings	2,500	10.3%
Brochures, stuffers, catalog listings	2,000	8.2%
American Bookseller ads	1.500	6.2%
Library Journal ads	1,000	4.1%
Baker & Taylor ads	1,000	4.1%
Ingram ads	1,000	4.1%
Mass mailings to key ABA stores	1,000	4.1%
Microfiche listings	800	3.3%
Telemarketing to key accounts	500	2.1%
	$24,300	100.0%

MAJOR SALES SOURCES: COMPANY SALES FORCE, OUTSIDE REPS, DISTRIBUTORS

A question on the survey was designed to help answer the question: *what percentage of sales for a typical publisher is derived from (A) its own sales reps and telemarketers, (B) outside sales reps or rep groups, (C) jobbers and distributors, and (D) other sales sources.*

Answers from the different publishing firms varied widely, as would be expected, depending on the divergent marketing approaches they have adopted. But the overall average may be taken as at least a partial indication of the overall sales approaches of the book industry for the present time:

Percentage of Sales Generated by Major Sales Sources

Sales Generated by	Percent
Company's own reps & telemarketers	40.9%
Outside reps or rep groups	26.4%
Jobbers and distributors	25.9%
Other	6.8%
	100.0%

BREAK-EVEN POINT FOR SALES REPRESENTATIVES

Another question addressed the yield required by a company to maintain a sales representative as a Company employee. The question was, "*What is the minimum sales per year a full-time sales rep must generate for your firm to reach his break-even point and be kept on the payroll?*"

Answers for this question broke down into two distinct groupings which separated the small from the large companies. The range for the *small companies* was from a low of $150,000 to a high of $500,000, with the ***mean*** falling at $316,666.

The range for *larger firms* extended from $1,000,000 to $2,000,000, with a ***mean*** of ***$1,416,666***.

The combined mean sales rep break-even point for all sizes of companies was ***$683,333***.

PERCENT OF A BOOK'S RETAIL PRICE SPENT ON ADVERTISING

Several questions on the survey were intended to analyze industry marketing expenditures per book sold. One of those questions read, "*If a book retails for $20.00, how much per book does your company allocate for advertising and marketing expenses (excluding salaries and commissions)?*"

The answers provided in dollars were converted into percentages. The ***mean*** score for advertising spent on a per-book basis was ***6.08%*** of the book's retail price. The range was from a minimum of 5% up to a maximum of 10%.

The most common answer provided, by far, was "***a dollar a book***." In discussing this figure with the survey participants, they several times commented that this was somewhat of an industry "rule of thumb," and that it applied to most books priced in the $15 to $25 retail price range.

TIMING OF BOOK-ADVERTISING EXPENDITURES

Another question of the survey asked, "*What percent of your company's advertising, promotion, and marketing budget for a typical book is spent before the book is released, during the product life cycle introductory stage, during the product life cycle growth stage, during the product life cycle maturity stage, and during the product life cycle decline stage?*"

The answers are summarized as follows:

Timing of Book Advertising Expenditures

% of Advertising	Product Life Cycle Stage
36.00%	Before release of the book
41.77%	During the life cycle *introductory* stage
16.45%	During the life cycle *growth* stage
5.78%	During the life cycle *maturity* stage
100.00%	

The range covering the percentage of advertising budget to be spent *before the book is released* extended from a minimum of 10% to a maximum of 80%, with a ***median*** of ***25%***. The suggested percents were quite evenly distributed throughout the range.

The range covering the percentage of advertising budget to be spent during the book's *introductory stage* was also quite evenly distributed, from the minimum of 10% to the maximum of 85%, with ***40%*** being the ***median***.

The range on advertising during the book's *growth stage* was more limited, from a minimum of 2% to a maximum of 50%.

"PUSH" VS. "PULL" ADVERTISING

Another question asked the publishers to *divide all their firm's advertising expenditures into two general categories: advertising directed to stores and institutional buyers who would, in turn, resell the goods to end users; versus advertising directed to end consumers.*

Advertising directed to stores was termed "*push*" advertising; advertising directed to the end consumers was considered "*pull*" advertising.

The survey showed that ***"push" advertising was slightly preferred to "pull" advertising,*** with a ***mean*** of ***52.68%***. The range was broad, however, with "push" advertising occupying 100% of the ad budget in some firms, down to as little as 10% in other companies. A histogram prepared indicated that the variation in budget devoted to"push" advertising was quite evenly spread, with at least one surveyed publisher at each of the ten levels indicated.

Since this question required that the combined "push" and "pull" advertising total 100%, "pull" advertising directed to the end users was credited with receiving ***47.32%*** of the composite advertising budget.

It should be noted that many of the firms showed their expenditures to be as widely differentiated as 75 and 25 percent, or 70 and 30 percent, or 60 and 40 percent, for the two types of advertising. Typically, each of the companies has adopted its own marketing plan based on the predominant use of either the "push" or "pull" approach.

Though the averages of the two types appear to be almost equal, such an equal advertising budget division is not representative of most of the companies surveyed. They were predominantly committed to either a "push" advertising stance or to the "pull" philosophy.

One observation should be made: the large publishers who are typically the producers of the nation's top "best-sellers" tend very strongly towards "push" advertising. Those companies who mainly stress the strength of their back lists typically use more "pull" advertising.

SUMMARY

In summary, the survey reveals a strong predisposition among the nation's publishers to advance and pre-release selling, product life cycles where over 90% of a book's total copies are sold during the first year, and expenditure of most of the book's advertising budget before the book reaches the stores and/or in the first two months of the book's existence.

Those publishers who anticipate longer product lives for their books, and who do little advance selling, typically realize lesser sales than those geared to a strong initial "push" effort.

9

How Authors Are Compensated: Royalty Policies

THE SWITCH FROM LIST-PRICE TO NET-RECEIPTS CALCULATIONS

Two decades ago, almost all royalties were calculated on the "list price" method. Now that approach has been abandoned by most publishers.

A major source of information on book-industry practices for many years has been an annual survey taken by a respected consulting firm: the Huenefeld Company. In the annual survey report which it produced in the spring of 1998, the Huenefeld Company summarized the practices of 155 mostly medium-sized U.S. publishers for the calendar year 1997. The report provides interesting data on the way book royalties are currently being paid to authors.

First of all, the report showed that 20% of the reporting publishers did not pay royalties. These companies apparently were reproducing in-house publications or were publishing on a buy-out basis.

Of more importance in this context is the report's information concerning the 80% of the companies they surveyed which do pay royalties. These companies are perceived as being typical of the vast majority of U.S. publishers, and their practices are indicative of how royalties are typically paid in the book-publishing industry today.

The Huenefeld Company report indicates that publishers presently calculate royalties in two different ways: (1) based on the net receipts which a book generates and (2) on the established retail price (the "list price") of the book. The invention of the computer, and the accompanying advent of computerized bookkeeping, allowed publishers to track to the penny the income and expenses related to each book they published. They quickly gained an awareness of relative costs and values. This computer tracking process began the shift from royalties based on list prices to royalties calculated on net receipts. In less than two decades, more than three-quarters of the commercial publishers have made the change, and the percentage of those who have done so appears to increase every year. It is a safe projection to estimate that within the next decade, almost all book royalties will be calculated and paid on a net receipts basis rather than a list price basis.

According to the Huenefeld report, 85.5% of the publishers surveyed for the year 1997 which pay royalties based their royalty payments to authors on net receipts generated by the author's book. Only 14.5% of the publishers based their royalties to authors on the list price of the book.

CURRENT STATISTICS ON ROYALTY RATES

How much royalty did the publishers pay? The report showed that the average royalty paid, based on ***net receipts***, was ***10.4%*** of the gross income received from the book. (In other words, if a book had a list price of $20.00, but was sold at a 40% discount, the publisher received $12.00 for the book. This $12.00 is the gross income for the book, and the figure upon which royalties are calculated according to this method.)

The report showed that for the year 1997, the average royalty paid, based on the book's ***list price***, was ***8.7%*** of the book's full retail value.

Many royalty structures pay different percentages based on the discounts which customers and bookstores receive when purchasing the books. Thus, full royalty might be paid on books sold at zero to 40% discount; perhaps three-fourths of full royalty for books sold at 41% to 44% discount; and perhaps half royalty for books sold at 45% or greater discounts. The royalty percentages will vary from publisher to publisher, and also from book to book. What is occurring in these percentage reductions is the publisher requiring the author to share proportionately in the reduced profits caused by the need to extend higher discounts to larger chains.

It should be noted that the royalty figures reported in this chapter are averages which mix unknown, first-time authors with established authors who have written numerous books and may be the authors of nationally known best-sellers.

Authors negotiating royalties on their first books most likely will receive offers at somewhat lower percentages than the average rates cited in this chapter. A royalty of 8% of net receipts is not uncommon for a first-time royalty for a new, unknown author.

HIGHEST ROYALTIES PAID

The Huenefeld survey report for 1997 also reported the highest royalties paid by all the reporting publishers. The figures below indicate the collective averages of the top royalty rates which the surveyed publishers reported paying.

The average highest royalty paid by publishers who pay royalties based on ***net receipts*** in 1997 was ***14.1%*** of net income received from the book.

The average highest royalty paid by publishers who paid royalties based on a book's ***list price*** in 1997 was ***11.5%*** of the book's list price.

ROYALTY ADVANCES

The 1997 Huenefeld Report previously cited in this chapter indicates that 64.5 percent of the publishers surveyed do not pay any royalty advances. Of the 35.5% who do pay royalty advances, the average advance they paid in 1997 was ***$2,747.00***.

The paying of royalty advances, especially to unknown and inexperienced authors, is increasingly rare. The dollar amounts of the advances paid is decreasing, and the number of authors receiving such advances is definitely declining.

The very large royalty advances occasionally reported in the media are, without exception, payments for nationally known individuals with a unique story to tell, and for nationally known authors of previous best-sellers where the expectation is that the forthcoming work will have similar reception to past works. Such large royalty advances are often the result of bidding wars between major publishers. These best-selling authors are the Michael Jordans, the Karl Malones, and the Steve Youngs of the writing industry. What they draw is far from typical of what the rest of the aspiring authors, who are mere mortals, can anticipate.

PRE-PUBLICATION BOOK PURCHASES

Some books are purchased outright by publishers in a lump-sum transaction, rather than reimbursing the author through semi-annual royalties. This procedure is sometimes used on books which the publisher believes will only yield marginal sales, with the purchase price at close to magazine-rate prices. Though many authors obviously prefer to receive more advantageous remuneration, this arrangement at least gets their book into print, where otherwise they would have no sale at all.

The publishers' objectives, in buy-out situations such as this, include such factors as (1) reducing potential risk of loss, (2) avoiding commitments to ongoing royalty computations on books which will probably have relatively low on-going sales, (3) bringing the book in-house for rewriting rather than having to spend long hours working with an inexperienced author, and (4) obtaining the book for use as a "filler" to round out the publisher's palette of new releases.

END-OF-RUN BOOK BUYOUTS

Sometimes, when sales of a book have slowed to the level that the book's sales during the coming one/two years will probably fall below the publisher's minimum monthly sales requirements, there is in-house debate as to whether to reprint the book or not. In such situations, publishers sometimes propose to the author a buyout arrangement for a modest sum with the commitment to keep the book in print for at least one more reprint edition. Obviously, what the publisher is seeking to do is to lower his break-even level on the reprint edition quantity, trying to justify a possible decision to reprint a small rerun. Though this arrangement results in a reduced royalty to the author, it provides him/her some income, and keeps the book in circulation for an extended period rather than allowing it to go out of print and pass into oblivion. Accepting such an offer is probably in the author's best interests. The chances of finding some other publisher to reprint a book which has gone out of print for lack of sales is almost nil.

ROYALTY ESCALATION CLAUSES

Sometimes a royalty escalation clause can be negotiated in which the royalty percentage increases after a certain quantity of books (perhaps 10,000 or 15,000 copies) have been sold. This is rarely done with first-time authors. Obviously, many books never achieve the designated number of sales stipulated in such clauses.

ROYALTIES FOR SALES TO BOOK CLUBS

Typical royalty contracts offer a royalty rate of 50% or less of full royalties for sales to book clubs. This is because book clubs either require and receive very deep discounts or they require very expensive advertising on the part of the publisher. The lower royalty rate on book club sales is clearly justified, and the publisher in reality may not be making anything at all on the book club transaction, and is using the book club offering primarily to meet its advertising objectives—calling the attention of many people nationwide to the existence of the book.

ROYALTIES FOR MASS MARKET PAPERBACK SALES

The printing or reprinting of a book as a mass-market paperback requires a very large print run, a relatively low retail price, access to national paperback distribution sources, and a very saleable book with national sales potential. Major mass market paperback publishers often won't consider reprinting another publisher's book unless it has already sold 100,000 or more copies in its original editions. Returns are not accepted by many mass-market paperback publishers and distributors—instead, the covers are torn off and submitted for return credit. This, of course, makes the book unsaleable. All these factors combine to make royalty payments on mass market paperbacks quite low and the probability of a book's never even being considered as a mass market candidate quite high.

10

Negotiating a Contract for Your Book

FORTY ITEMS A PUBLISHING CONTRACT SHOULD SPECIFY

Book publishing contracts come in many forms and styles. If you are entering into a contract with a bona fide book publishing company for the publication of your manuscript, your contract will probably deal with all of the following areas. You can use this list as a checklist.

1. The company's name and address.
2. Your name, address, telephone number, year of birth, and social security number.
3. The tentative, or working title for your book, and subtitle, if any.
4. Your granting of the rights to publish and sell your manuscript to the publisher.
5. The territorial rights covered by your publishing grant (usually world-wide).
6. The language rights covered by your publishing grant (usually all languages).
7. Who has the right to determine the title, format, style, type, illustrations, size, paper, printing, binding, cover design, date of publication, sale price, terms and conditions of sales, etc., of the book (usually the publisher).
8. The author's commitment to not print or publish any other edition of the book, or any book of a similar nature, or do anything which might interfere with or injure the sale of the book without the publisher's written consent.
9. Who is to own the copyright and to file with the U.S. Register of Copyrights to obtain the copyright. (Usually the publisher files it, since a copyright is actually the right to produce and distribute the book for profit. If an author chooses to retain ownership of the copyright on his book, the publisher will, of necessity, take away from the author the right to produce and distribute the book, elsewhere in the contract.)
10. The author's guarantee that the work contains no libelous or plagiarized materials, and his guarantee that in the event a lawsuit is launched against the publisher and/or author asserting that the book is libelous or in breach of

copyright in any way, he (the author) will be responsible for the payment of all legal defense costs.

11. The author's commitment to provide a completed manuscript to the publisher by a certain date, in the form or forms which the contract specifies.

12. Agreement as to what will happen if the manuscript is not submitted by the specified date.

13. Agreement as to who is to edit, proofread, index, provide artwork for, and accomplish other tasks required to make the book ready for publication.

14. Agreement as to who will pay for expenses caused by author's changes to the book after the book has been submitted, including how and when those expenses will be paid.

15. Agreement as to what the author's obligation is concerning the reading and correcting of the publisher's typeset proofs.

16. Agreement as to who will pay for changes requested by the author in subsequent editions of the book (usually the author).

17. Agreement as to what marketing assistance the author will provide, if any.

18. Agreement as to what will happen if the book is not published by the agreed-upon or projected publication date.

19. Agreement concerning any free copies which the publisher may furnish to the author, if any.

20. Agreement concerning the author's right to purchase copies of his book, and other items which the publisher produces, including discount rates and required time of payment.

21. Agreement concerning the withholding of author's debts to the publisher from royalties, if such exist when royalties come due.

22. Agreement concerning the author's obligation to pay service charges and legal collection costs if he incurs indebtedness to the publisher and does not pay on time.

23. Agreement concerning the rate(s) of royalties which the publisher will pay to the author.

24. Agreement as to the due date of royalties to be paid by the publisher to the author, and as to the months' sales which are included for payments in those periodic royalty payments,

including the providing of financial statements pertaining to the sales of the book.

25. Agreement concerning whether royalties are to be paid on books given to the author, travelers' samples, damaged copies, review copies, free bonus copies, books sold but not paid for. (Royalties are usually not paid on these items.)

26. The author's granting to the publisher of rights to negotiate subsidiary rights sales and licenses to reprint the book to other publishers, including foreign-language editions, book clubs, periodical publications, computer disk editions, audio and video recordings, dramatic productions and TV and stage production rights.

27. Agreement as to the rate of reimbursement to the author for subsidiary rights sales made by the publisher.

28. Agreement concerning the rate of payment to the author for copies of the book sold through book clubs.

29. Agreement concerning the rate of payment to the author if the book is reproduced in mass market paperback format, either by the publisher or another licensed publisher.

30. Agreement to the author's rights to have the publisher's books audited on any matters which pertain to the author's book and income therefrom (usually performed at the author's expense).

31. A definition as to how long the publishing agreement will remain in force, and how it can be terminated.

32. Agreement concerning notification obligations of the author's heirs, in case of his death, in order to keep the publisher's obligation to pay royalties in force.

33. Agreement concerning the rights of the publisher, and of the author, to transfer their respective interests in the book to other parties.

34. Agreement concerning what will happen to the book and the author's rights concerning payments due and concerning the copyright and ownership of the book in the event the publisher discontinues the publishing operation.

35. Agreement concerning what happens to the book and concerning the copyright and ownership of the book in the event the publisher elects to let the book go out of print, or elects to remainder remaining copies on hand.

36. Agreement concerning how disputes are to be resolved in the event they arise between the author and the publisher.

37. The author's granting of an option on his forthcoming works to the publisher, if any option is to be granted, with stipulations concerning competitive bidding and publisher's rights to match competitors' offers, etc.

38. Agreement as to the tentative publication date of the book.

39. Other provisions to which all parties agree concerning the publication of the book.

40. A clause indicating that the contract constitutes the complete agreement of the negotiating parties.

Though other clauses may find their way into very sophisticated contracts, these are the basic items which should be contained in a typical contract negotiation.

It is suggested that new authors, when they finally reach that glorious day when they have their first book publication contract to "look over," should compare their contract with this checklist to be sure all the essential elements are covered.

A SAMPLE BOOK PUBLICATION CONTRACT

The rest of this chapter is a reproduction of a typical book publication contract. Like most publishers' contracts, this document has been compiled from a variety of different sources. This one is drawn from portions of the contracts currently being utilized by several major companies involved in either trade or religious publishing, or both. It effectively addresses the 40 items on the preceding checklist which are essential elements of a publication negotiation and agreement.

As you read the contract, note that it basically is divided into two sections. The first portion, in essence, defines the terms of the agreement and protects the publisher's interests. The latter portion primarily serves to protect the author's interests. In total, it is a balanced, comprehensive document and a model which both authors and publishers can utilize as they solidify their mutual agreements.

ABC Book Publishers'
PUBLICATION CONTRACT

An agreement dated __________, between ABC Book Publishers, Inc. (hereafter referred to as the "Publisher") and the author,

Author's name: John J. Doe
Address: 123 Main Street,
Writers' Roost, US 55555
Home Telephone: (111) 111-1111
Work Telephone: (111) 222-2222
Year of Birth: 1964
Social Security Number: 000-00-0000

(hereafter referred to as the "Author") for rights to publish, distribute, and to license subsequent publication or other utilization by others of a written manuscript at present tentatively entitled

How to Write Nifty Novels

(hereafter referred to as the "Work").

1. Publication and Distribution Rights. The Author hereby grants to the Publisher exclusive right to publish and sell said Work, or any revised, enlarged or abridged edition thereof, in any appropriate book format(s), in the English language and in non-English languages, in the United States of America, Canada, and all other areas of the world.

The Publisher shall have the sole right to determine the title, format, and style of the Work, and to select type, illustrations, paper, printing, binding, and other manufacturing materials and specifications it believes best suited for the Work. The Publisher shall further be entitled to promote or advertise the Work in a manner it deems appropriate, and shall be entitled to determine the date of publication, the sale price, and all terms and conditions of sale.

During the period of this contract, the Author will not, without the written consent of the Publisher, write, print, or publish any other edition of the Work, or any other work of a similar character, or a work that could be considered another of the same series, or which is reasonably likely to or does interfere with or injure the sale of the Work, nor will the Author permit the use of his name on or in connection with the publication of any such work.

2. Copyright. It is understood and agreed that the copyright shall be filed with the U.S. Register of Copyrights in the name of the Publisher, and the Publisher is hereby authorized to take all steps required to secure said copyright in the United States and in such other countries as may be covered by this agreement. If no copyright be obtained, for any reason, the Author grants the Publisher exclusive right to publish the Work, according to the terms of this contract, for a period of fifty (50) years.

3. Legal Responsibility for Content. The Author guarantees and represents that the said Work is innocent and contains no matter libelous or otherwise unlawful; that the said Work in no wise infringes upon the copyright or violates the right of privacy or any other right of any person or party whatsoever; that he is the sole author, proprietor, or creator of the said Work and has full power to make this agreement and grant, and that the said Work is original and not in the public domain.

The author guarantees that he will indemnify and hold harmless the Publisher against any suit, claim, demand or recovery, by judgment finally sustained, by reason of any violation of proprietary right or copyright by, or any unlawful matter contained in, the said Work. In the event any legal action is brought against the Publisher for any violation or alleged violation of a proprietary right or copyright by, or any unlawful matter contained in, the said Work, the Publisher shall have the right, at the expense of the Author, to defend, through counsel of its own choosing, any suit involving any of the matters herein referred to. The Author agrees to pay all attorneys' fees, court costs, and any other costs incurred by the Publisher in connection with the legal action.

4. Manuscript Completion Date. The Author agrees to provide a completed manuscript of said Work, conforming in all essential respects to the concept of the Work represented to the Publisher on the date of this agreement, and acceptable in style and content to the Publisher, no later than __________.

The Author further agrees to provide such photographs, illustrations, and other supplemental material as shall have been included in that prior concept of the work, and permission for any inclusion of material copyrighted by others, at the Author's expense, no later than ___________.

Unless otherwise agreed in this contract, the Author is to provide the finished manuscript to the Publisher in both double-spaced computer printout and computer word-processing disk form. The computer files shall be in WordPerfect (preferably version 6.0 for DOS or 6.1 for Windows), on a 3½" high density disk or disks, spell-checked, suitable for printing on an IBM computer. Word-processing programs other than WordPerfect may also be used, with prior permission from the Publisher.

In the event the manuscript is not provided to the Publisher by the said date, the Publisher may exercise the option of either extending this manuscript completion date or terminating this agreement.

The Author agrees to make any changes deemed necessary and desirable by the Publisher, and to prepare a table of contents, an index, footnotes, appendices, and bibliography, if they are requested by the Publisher. In the event of the Author's failure to do so promptly and satisfactorily, the Publisher may prepare such materials or make such changes and charge the cost thereof to the Author, or charge the cost against royalties due.

In the absence of a written request from the Author prior to publication for its return, the Publisher, after publication of the Work, may dispose of the original manuscript. Except for loss or damage due to its own negligence, the Publisher shall not be responsible for loss or damage to any property of the Author.

5. Proofs and Author Changes. Prior to publication of the said Work, the Publisher shall provide to the Author one set of proofs of the typographical composition of the Work, and shall agree to correct any typographical errors and other discrepancies between said proofs and the final edited version of the original manuscript at no cost to the Author. The Author agrees to read and indicate corrections in the proofs and return them to the Publisher within seven (7) days after receiving them.

Additional changes and rewriting instituted by the Author in the proofs will be made only if acceptable to both Author and Publisher. The cost of such changes as are proposed by the Author are to be paid by the Author, or deducted from subsequent royalties due the Author if the Publisher and Author so agree in writing before the changes are made.

Author-requested changes in subsequent editions shall be made at the Author's expense, and payment to the Publisher shall be made by the Author within fifteen (15) days of publication of the new edition.

6. Author's Marketing Assistance. The Author agrees to assist in the publishing and marketing of the Work by completing for the Publisher a questionnaire giving details of the Author's background and qualifications; by providing photographs of the Author for publicity purposes; by writing suggested "About the Book" and "About the Author" flap copy; by providing potential customer address lists and other helpful information; and by making personal appearances to assist in effective marketing of the Work.

7. Publication Date. The Publisher agrees to publish the said Work at its own expense, in such style as it deems best suited to its sale. The Publisher further agrees to publish said Work and offer it for sale on or before the time designated in this contract, or within no more than one year after such date.

In the event said Work is not published and offered for sale, in book form, within that period, the Author may exercise the option of either extending said publication date or terminating this agreement.

8. Author Copies, Discounts and Payments. The Publisher agrees to present to the Author ten (10) finished copies of the Work upon publication without charge, and to permit the Author to purchase further copies for his own personal use at the Publisher's current wholesale discount schedule (___% discount).

The Author may purchase his books in quantities of one hundred (100) at a time at a ___% discount, two hundred (200) at a time at a ___% discount, or three hundred (300) or more at a time at a ___% discount, to be paid for at the time of purchase and arranged for in advance with the Publisher.

The Author may also purchase copies of all other books published and/or regularly stocked on a wholesale basis by ABC Publishers, Inc., at the then-current wholesale discount schedule (typically 40% discount).

The Author's purchases are to be paid for as books are obtained unless he has completed and submitted a credit application which has been accepted by ABC Publishers, Inc. If credit is extended by ABC Publishers, Inc., the Author agrees to make full payment within thirty (30) days of the date of the invoice. In the event payment is not made by the Author within thirty (30) days, the Author agrees to pay service charges and any necessary collection charges (including collection fees, legal fees, and forfeiture of wholesale discounts) as stipulated in the Publisher's then-current wholesale trade terms and/or the Author's signed credit application.

The Publisher is authorized by this contract to withhold any amount payable on account by the Author to the Publisher, including service charges on unpaid invoices, from royalty payments due and payable to the Author by the Publisher.

9. Royalties. The Publisher agrees to pay to the Author, or his duly authorized representative, a royalty of:

____

____

____

It is understood that royalties will not be paid on copies given to the Author, travelers' samples, damaged copies, free bonus copies, and copies given away for review or for the purpose of aiding the sale of the Work.

Books are not considered sold until they are paid for in full by the purchaser(s). Royalties are not paid for books sold on invoices which are written off as bad debts because of customer non-payment. In the event a purchaser defaults on payment to the Publisher for copies purchased of the Author's Work, royalties for said copies will be withheld unless and until payment in full is received. In such cases, unpaid royalties will be paid in the next scheduled royalty payment.

10. Subsidiary Rights. The Author hereby grants to the Publisher exclusive rights to license others to publish subsequent editions of the Work in the English language in all areas included in this agreement, and to license others to publish the Work in translation in all such areas. The Author hereby grants to the Publisher exclusive rights to license others to publish subsequent editions of the Work in the English language and in foreign-language translations in all areas included in this agreement. These subsequent editions by other parties include book club editions; mass market paperback reprints; condensed and abridged versions, including selections of the Work in anthologies and similar publications; periodical publications (including magazines, newspapers and digests); audio, video tape or CD recordings; computer disk editions; computer or filmstrip productions; filmstrips; printed cartoon versions and mechanical reproductions. The Publisher agrees to pay to the Author a royalty amounting to ___% of all monies received by said Publisher from such licensing arrangements to others.

In the event terms of licensing to a book club or other individual or firm include provision for the Publisher to provide printed copies at a specific production cost, said production cost shall be deducted from monies received prior to calculation of the royalty due the Author.

The Author grants the Publisher exclusive rights to license others to produce adaptations of the Work in dramatic productions including stage plays, radio productions, television productions, movie productions, and other stage, screen, cinema and dramatic works. The Publisher agrees to pay to the Author a royalty amounting to ___% of all monies received by said publisher from such licensing arrangements to others.

The Publisher may, at its discretion and without thereby incurring any liability to the Author, publish or permit others to publish any selections of the Work which the Publisher may deem appropriate to promote the sales of the Work. In the event that the Publisher receives no compensation from the publication of such editions, it shall be under no obligation to the Author with respect thereto.

The Publisher may allow Braille or sight-saving editions or "talking books" for the blind to be made or published. In the event that the Publisher receives no compensation from the publication of such editions, it shall be under no obligation to the Author with respect thereto.

11. Royalty Payments and Accounting. The Publisher agrees to render, on the _____ day of __________ and on the _____ day of __________, in each year, semi-annual statements of the amount of sales (less authorized returns) for the six-month period ending on the last day of the month preceding by ninety (90) days said accounting dates.

Payment of all royalties for the above-described six-month periods due the Author, after subtraction of previously paid advances, typographical alteration costs, or other indebtedness to the Publisher for which the Author is liable, shall be made in full at the time of each such accounting unless other terms of payment have been accepted prior to said accounting by both Author and Publisher.

Statements and payments shall be mailed to the last-known address of the Author. If statements fail to reach the Author, the Publisher agrees to furnish duplicate statements on request. The Author agrees to notify the publisher of changes in his mailing address within thirty (30) days.

12. Book Clubs and Promotional Programs. The Publisher may, at its election, distribute and sell copies of the

Work through book promotional sales programs such as book clubs owned either by the Publisher or by other contractual agents, in which books sold may be discounted to the purchaser for continuing or quantity purchases. Should it so elect, the Publisher agrees to pay, and the Author agrees to accept, a royalty on such sales of ________ percent (___%) of net book club sales.

13. Mass Market Editions. It is understood and agreed that after one year from the date of publication of the Work, the Publisher may publish a "cheap" or mass-market edition of said Work, and that he shall pay to the Author, according to the royalty payment schedule previously established, a royalty for each copy sold of _________ percent (___%) of net mass market edition sales.

14. Accounting Auditing. The Author or his authorized representative shall have the right, upon written request, to examine the books of account of the Publisher, in so far as they relate to the said Work. The cost of said examination, if any, shall be at the expense of the Author.

15. Duration of Contract Obligation. This agreement shall be binding on both Author and Publisher and upon their respective heirs, administrators, successors and assigns, for as long as a registered copyright to said Work, including renewals and extensions, remains in force, unless terminated by written agreement of all parties, or as specifically provided for elsewhere in this agreement. If no copyright be obtained, for any reason, the duration of this contract shall be for a period of fifty (50) years.

Both the Publisher and the Author, or their heirs, are to notify the other party of any change which would affect the distribution of any royalty payment or other transaction within ninety (90) days of the occurrence of such change. In the event of the death of the Author, the payment of royalties to the estate of the deceased is to be permanently terminated by the Publisher unless a written application for royalty continuance is made to the Publisher by an authorized administrator of the estate within three months of the Author's death, or unless prior written instructions for the royalty continuance to his heirs or estate have been made by the Author and filed with the Publisher.

16. Transfer of Rights to Other Parties. The Author shall be entitled to assign or transfer his rights to receive royalty payments by written notice to the Publisher. No such assignments or transfers shall be effective until the Publisher shall receive written notice from the Author. The rights of any assignee shall be subject to the rights of the Publisher under this agreement.

The Publisher may transfer or sell the copyright and/or publication rights of the Work to another party, providing that party agrees to provide semi-annual reports and pay a royalty amounting to the original royalty percents to the Author on the same schedule as agreed upon in this contract.

17. Discontinuation of Publishing Operation. In the event of permanent discontinuation of publishing operations by the Publisher without previous sale of rights concerning the Work to a third party, whether as a result of bankruptcy or any other reason, all rights transferred to the Publisher by this agreement shall revert to the Author, including copyright ownership and the right to purchase negatives and/or typeset copy at cost from the Publisher to continue publication of the Work.

18. Discontinuation of Publication of the Work. In case the Publisher fails to keep the said Work in print and for sale and, after written demand from the Author, declines or neglects to reprint the Work within six months and to offer it for sale; or in case after two years from the date of first publication the said Work, in the opinion of the Publisher, is no longer marketable or profitable, and he gives notice to the Author, the Publisher's rights under this contract shall terminate and all rights granted under this agreement shall revert to the Author.

In the event the Publisher allows the Work to go out of print for more than six months, the publisher shall grant the Author the option to purchase the typeset copy, negatives and plates of the Work, and any remaining copies or sheets, at the manufacturing cost (including composition) of such plates and copies of sheets, in default of which purchase the Publisher shall have the right to destroy any typeset copy, negatives and plates and sell any copies at cost or less without payment of royalty to the Author upon such sales.

19. Arbitration of Disputes. Any dispute between the parties to this agreement which involves interpretation of the terms of this or subsequent agreements shall be submitted to arbitration under the rules of the American Arbitration Association, and the findings of the Arbitrator shall be binding on all parties.

Any other dispute concerning fulfillment of this agreement shall be litigated in a court of competent jurisdiction, in the state in which the Publisher's office facility is located. Legal interpretation of this agreement shall be governed by the laws of the state in which the Publisher is incorporated.

20. Option for Next Works. The Author agrees to submit to the Publisher his next two book-length works in the same general subject-matter area and/or works written to the same general audience or market, before submitting the same to any other publisher. The Publisher shall be entitled to a period of twelve (12) weeks after the submission of the completed manuscript within which to notify the Author of its publication decision. If within that time the Publisher shall notify the Author of its desire to publish the manuscript, the Publisher shall thereupon negotiate with the Author with respect to the terms of such publication.

If within thirty (30) days thereafter the parties are unable to arrive in good faith at a mutually satisfactory agreement for such publication, the Author shall be free to submit his manuscript elsewhere, provided, however, that he shall not enter into a contract for the publication of such manuscript with any other publisher upon terms less favorable than those offered by the Publisher, and provided that the Publisher has the option of matching the royalty payment terms offered by the competing party.

21. Tentative Publication Date. The tentative publication period of the Work, as scheduled by the Publisher, is ____________________ through ____________________.

22. Other Provisions. Other provisions agreed to by all parties are: ____

____

____

____

____

____

____

____

23. Complete Agreement. This agreement constitutes the complete understanding of the parties. No modification or waiver of any provision shall be valid unless in writing and signed by both parties, and attached to all copies of this contract.

In witness whereof the parties hereunto set their hands.

________________________	________________________
Witness	Author/Compiler
________________________	________________________
Witness	Publisher

11

Observations on Book Pricing

PROFITABILITY: A PERENNIAL CHALLENGE WHEN CHOOSING AND PRICING BOOKS FOR PUBLICATION

What's the correct retail price for a book? An adequate reply for this simple question is a very complex challenge.

The basic requirement, from a publisher's perspective, is that the book must yield sufficient income to pay for

1. The costs of the book's composition and manufacture,
2. The cost of the author's royalties,
3. The costs of warehousing, invoicing, and shipping the books,
4. The costs of advertising and marketing the book,
5. The cost of sales commissions to the publisher's sales representatives, to outside reps, and to telemarketers,
6. The book's share of the costs of plant overhead,
7. The costs of shrinkage due to returns, damaged and defective books,
8. The costs of collecting and processing the invoices involving sales and returns of the book, including write-offs for bad debts,
9. The reduction of profits caused by the need to extend higher than normal (can we say "exorbitant"?) discounts to chain-stores and jobbers,
10. The time value of money for the time the book sits on the shelves, and the value costs of lost opportunity to invest in a more profitable investment, if the book proves to be a slow mover, and
11. Profit, after taxes are paid, on the amount of income from the book which exceeds all of the above costs.

PUBLISHING IS SELECTIVE INVESTING

There is considerable risk in investing in a new book's publication. Many a publisher has several years' supplies of books on hand in the warehouse for which the sales failed to meet expectations and projections.

Investing in publishing is, in many ways, like investing in the stock market. Just as some stocks yield better than others, some books also yield better than other publications. Profitability often hinges on the publisher's expertise in picking the "winners."

When an author approaches a publisher with the solicitation to publish his manuscript, he is really saying to the publisher, "Invest in my project." If authors better understood that relationship, their queries and proposals would immediately improve in quality, and so would their manuscripts.

THE ONE-YEAR SALES WINDOW

The publisher's objective, for an average-selling book, usually is to print the quantity of books which can be sold profitably within a one-year period, and then to reprint as necessary, using the same one-year sales-window guideline to help him determine whether the book should be reprinted. Initial print runs are often cautiously determined, with the intent of reprinting the new book during the first year if the book is on track with sales projections, and considering the reprint as an extension of the initial print run.

CHANGES IN DISCOUNT STRUCTURES ARE DRIVING LIST PRICES HIGHER

A dramatic change in the retail price of books, which has occurred primarily during the past two decades, is the escalation in list prices caused by the discounting practices of large chain stores. These stores, knowing that they plan to discount the books they purchase, seek very high discounts, longer payment times, free freight, free return privileges, and other concessions. To maintain their necessary margins, publishers have inflated the list prices on their books to still maintain the necessary income level they must receive for the book.

Thus, the average list price for newly published paperbacks has escalated dramatically. Evidence for this is found, for instance, in the Huenefeld Company's report, for the 155 publishers it surveyed for the year 1997. The average ***new paperback*** list price was ***$23.12***. This price varied among different types of publications. Thus, the average retail price for trade paperbacks produced by secular trade publishers was ***$19.26;*** for religious trade publishers it was only ***$12.93.***

Obviously, the religious trade publishers' figures are skewed by their emphasis on small, short books of the "Life's Little Instruction Books" genre.

The average list price for newly published hardbound books has escalated even more dramatically. The same report showed the average ***hardbound*** price to be ***$54.83***, with secular trade publishers' hardbound books averaging to ***$41.23*** and the religious trade publishers' hardcover books averaging to ***$21.89***.

DRAMATIC SHIFTS FROM HARDCOVER TO TRADE PAPERBACK FORMATS

Because of the increasing price levels, there has been a dramatic shift from hardbound to trade paperback format in the publishing world. The 155 publishers surveyed in the above-mentioned information reported that only ***25.7*** percent of their books were published in ***hardcover editions***. That percentage was ***36.6*** percent for secular trade publishers, but only a tiny ***9.5*** percent for the religious trade publishers.

Thus, when the overall average number of new titles in 1997 for the surveyed publishers was 35, the typical publisher produced 26 paperbacks and nine hardcover books. The secular trade publishers averaged 41 new titles: 26 paperbacks and 15 hardcover books. In the religious trade area the average number of new titles was 42—38 paperbacks and only four hardbound books.

A BOOK PRODUCTION COST MODEL

A book production costing model has been developed for the overall sample reported in the above survey, then replicated for the secular trade area and religious trade area. The model's components are as follows:

1. Average print quantity: the average of the 155 publishers' new-book first-run print quantities.
2. The average number of pages in the books they produced.

3. The acquisition cost per page, then multiplied by the average number of pages to determine an overall acquisition cost.
4. The average cost of an externally created cover.
5. The average pre-press cost per page, for typesetting, proofreading, negatives, flats, and press plates; then multiplied by the average number of pages to determine an overall pre-press cost.
6. The printing and binding cost per page, then multiplied by the average number of pages to determine an overall printing and binding cost. (In this model, there is no distinction between paperback books and hardbound books with covers and jackets—they are all averaged together in the data supplied.) Then the total cost of printing and binding per book is multiplied by the average number of books in the print run to obtain a total printing and binding cost.
7. The totals of the above data, which yield a total production cost, a cost per book, and then a cost per page.
8. The average new paperback cover price, divided by the average number of pages to determine an average paperback price per page.
9. The average new hardbound book cover price, divided by the average number of pages to determine an average hardcover book price per page.

All the above data, for the total sample of reporting publishers, followed by the data for secular trade publishers and then for religious trade publishers, is reproduced on page 151, titled *Average Book Production Costs.*

THE EFFECTS OF SHORTER PRINT RUNS AND OTHER VARIABLES

But the above model is assuming quite a number of things which may not hold true from publisher to publisher. For instance, many may choose to utilize shorter press runs, which save on initial capital requirements and storage space, and also reduce the risk factor of having overprinted on what

AVERAGE BOOK PRODUCTION COSTS

	Total Sample		Secular Trade		Religious Trade	
Average print quantity	**5,770**		**5,829**		**6,949**	
Average pages	**217**		**214**		**184**	
Acquisition cost per page	$37.17		$31.72		$39.69	
Book's total acquisition cost		**8,065.89**		**6,788.08**		**7,302.96**
The average cost of an externally created cover		**1,056.00**		**921.00**		**1,225.00**
Average pre-press cost per page	$53.10		$44.52		$46.19	
Pre-press cost per book		**11,522.70**		**9,527.28**		**8,498.96**
Printing and binding cost per page	$.0094		$.0123		$.0074	
Printing and binding cost per book	$2.0398		$2.6322		$1.3616	
Printing and binding per press run		**11,769.65**		**15,343.09**		**9,461.76**
Total cost per press run		**$32,414.24**		**$32,579.45**		**$26,488.68**
Cost per book	$5.62		$5.59		$3.81	
Cost per page	$.0259		$.0261		$.0207	
Average new paperback cover price	**$23.12**		**$19.26**		**$12.93**	
Average paperback price per page	$.1065		$.0900		$.0703	
Average new hardback cover price	**$54.83**		**$41.23**		**$21.89**	
Average hardback price per page	$.2527		$.1927		$.1190	

may turn out to be a slow-moving book, but rapidly increases the cost per unit for printing and binding.

Other variations are obvious: a highly technical or scholarly book with extensive charts and footnotes will increase the typesetting and proofreading costs. Some books may require costly artwork which could double the cost of cover design. Some publishers pay higher printing prices than others. Some books contain very valuable information, but it is obvious that they appeal to only a very small audience—it may be worthwhile to publish them, but allowance will have to be made for the long time they will sit on the shelf before the run has sold out. Again, the time value of money becomes a factor in determining retail prices.

Many publishers use much shorter print runs than those reported as average print runs in the survey under consideration. For instance, while the overall average print run was reported as 5,770, the average ***shortest print quantity*** the same publishers reported was ***2,109*** copies (***2,590*** for secular trade publishers and ***2,701*** for religious trade publishers).

All these variations may increase the book production costs per page reported in the preceding chart significantly—perhaps even as much as 25 percent. Assuming such was the case, the overall cost per page for all reported publishers might increase to ***$.0324*** (to ***$.0326*** per page for secular trade publishers and to ***$.0259*** per page for religious trade publishers).

CURRENT PRICE-PER-PAGE BOOK PRICING

Analysis of the retail price per page currently being charged by a reasonable sample of publishers shows a broad variance. The two charts which follow show what per-page rates typical 6" x 9" books, with few photographs and without costly design features which would radically alter their production costs, are being priced at. The analysis is based on new-release catalogs and listings which flowed into the author's publishing and distributing operation during the early spring of 1998. Books in other formats, such as large-size picture books, or books utilizing internal color printing which

PER-PAGE PRICING ANALYSIS SPRING 1998 FORTHCOMING AND NEWLY-RELEASED BOOKS

6" x 9" Hardbound Books, with Jackets

Publisher	Number of Books	Average Cost per Page
Sourcebooks, Inc.	2	0.2073
Fordham University Press	5	0.1864
Dove Books	1	0.1864
Ohio University Press	4	0.1569
M.E. Sharpe, Inc.	3	0.1352
Northern Illinois University Press	2	0.1314
Upper Quartile		**0.1309**
Temple University Press	32	0.1305
Westminster John Knox Press	4	0.1303
Prometheus Books	9	0.1234
University of Minnesota Press	16	0.1205
Augsburg Fortress Press	5	0.1111
Liguori/Triumph Publications	1	0.1071
Median		**0.1019**
University of Nevada Press	22	0.0967
The Kent State University Press	5	0.0904
Avon Books	19	0.0901
Bard Mass Market (a division of Avon Books)	3	0.0898
MacMurray and Beck	6	0.0876
Covenant Communications	3	0.0780
Lower Quartile		**0.0774**
Bethany House Publishers	2	0.0769
Bookcraft, Inc.	12	0.0680
Horizon Publishers	6	0.0620
Deseret Book Company	16	0.0600
Morehouse Publishing	1	0.0568
Abingdon Press	2	0.0551
	Mean Cost Per Page:	**$0.1099**

PER-PAGE PRICING ANALYSIS
SPRING 1998
FORTHCOMING AND NEWLY-RELEASED BOOKS

6" x 9" Paperback Books

Publisher	Number of Books	Average Cost per Page
Ohio University Press	12	0.1393
Princeton Book Company Publishers	4	0.1250
Abingdon Press	8	0.0933
Sourcebooks, Inc.	6	0.0848
Fordham University Press	2	0.0846
Dove Books	4	0.0831
Upper Quartile		**0.0798**
Independent Publishers Group	2	0.0765
The AEI Press	2	0.0760
Avon Books	13	0.0754
Augsburg Fortress Publishers	22	0.0752
Westminster John Knox Press	32	0.0723
Horizon Publishers	4	0.0717
Northern Illinois University Press	2	0.0715
Median		**0.0713**
Temple University Press	14	0.0711
M.E. Sharpe, Inc.	2	0.0701
Morehouse Publishing	10	0.0675
Loyola Press	3	0.0675
Liguori/Triumph Publications	3	0.0641
Bookcraft, Inc.	3	0.0620
MacMurray & Beck	5	0.0619
Lower Quartile		**0.0618**
Prometheus Books	13	0.0618
Deseret Book Company	5	0.0590
Natural Resources	37	0.0529
The Kent State University Press	20	0.0494
Covenant Communications	15	0.0490
Bethany House Publishers	26	0.0404
	Mean Cost Per Page:	**$0.0733**

made them different from the typical black-and-white basic format of the publishing industry, have been excluded from the analysis.

After viewing the rates per page in these charts, it is obvious that rates vary widely for similar types of books and printing. Again, it is not the actual cost of the manufacturing of the books which is determining the price of the books, it is the other expenses which the publisher must meet: sales costs, advertising costs, salaries, overhead, extra discounts, high returns, and profit requirements. Publishers are no longer willing, nor able, to live on a substandard level to "hold the price down" for the reading public. They want their staffs to be adequately compensated, and they want to be able to enjoy reasonable personal income and corporate profit margins comparable with other industries. Those are the factors driving book prices upward, not the cost of manufacture of the books.

And one cannot set prices realistically by just counting pages. Books vary in innate value of their contents, subject matter, and quality of writing. Filet mignon sells for far more per pound than hamburger, yet they are both meat and beef. So it is with books—a retail price divided by the number of pages is not a realistic measurement. Allowance must be made for the unique compelling features which will entice customers to buy the book, and for the additional marketing expenses which are driving the book's continued sales.

DO CUSTOMERS SET PRICES?

Many authors, and many bookstore clerks, think they know what retail prices books should carry, but experience has shown that their opinions are usually woefully behind the times and not in tune with the rapid changes and trends which are characteristic of present-day book publishing.

Do customers (or authors, or bookstore clerks) set prices? John Huenefeld gave a realistic response to this question to the publishers he addressed in his semi-monthly newsletter, in an article titled, *Pricing to Weed Out Weak Books, and*

Make Strong Ones Support Your Budget (*The Huenefeld Report*, 9 March 1998). He wrote,

> When asked how they determine prices, a substantial portion of publishers say: "We price at what the market will bear." The first problem with that answer is that few publishers actually know what the market will bear. If their acquisition editors are consistent and disciplined about insisting that every book they contract or otherwise acquire has one or more "compelling unique features" not easily available elsewhere, readers will pay more for those features than most publishers assume.
>
> But what readers seem willing to pay (or what your closest competition is charging for similar books) is really beside the point. If properly estimated, that may determine the maximum price it's feasible to set—but not the minimum. Minimum prices need to be high enough to cover both the discounts you give trade middlemen, and each book's appropriate share of all of your publishing costs—and then contribute something to your desired operating ("profit") margin.
>
> If you believe a minimum price which does this is higher than readers will pay, it makes no sense to adjust the price downward (to match competition, or stay within what you think the market will bear). You'll probably lose money. You're better off simply deciding not to publish the book. . . .
>
> In a sense, pricing is the world's best literary critic.

12

Current Book Industry Trends

AN HISTORICAL COMPARISON: BOOK INDUSTRY BUSINESS TRENDS IN 1988

The 1988 survey of major publishers taken by the author of this work reported 15 significant trends observed by the major publishers. Their 1988 comments regarding changes they felt were impacting the industry are briefly summarized below to provide historical perspective. The next section of this chapter will comment in more detail on trends as they are observed a decade later, in 1998.

When asked to comment on the various book industry trends they had observed during the preceding year, the individuals interviewed in 1988 pointed to the following changes which they felt were impacting the industry:

1. ***Large publishers acquiring smaller publishing houses***. They perceived the merger and acquisition trend as continuing, with major firms acquiring still more clout as they broadened their publishing bases even wider.

2. ***Bookstore chains buying out independent bookstores***. The same merger mania was perceived as operating on the retail-store level, with local bookstores being absorbed into regional and nationwide operations.

3. ***Bookstore chains buying more from distributors***. Fewer small publishers were finding success in their efforts to place their books with major chain operations. They were being forced to take their wares to distributors for resale to the chains, which caused them to have to sell a greater percent of their books at deeper discounts. This in turn compelled them to place higher retail prices on their books in many instances.

4. ***More book distribution companies functioning***. There was more emphasis on a middle man between small publishers and major chain operations. These distributors, with their own networks of sales reps, were also carrying the sales representative responsibility for more of the smaller publishers.

5. ***More small, independent publishers entering the publishing arena***. The proliferation of new publishing firms at recent ABA conventions gave visible evidence of this trend.

6. ***Small, independent presses defining and filling niches well.*** With their more modest goals and better market targeting, they were taking display space away from medium-sized publishers, and those medium-sized generalists were being squeezed.

7. ***Publishers expanding into new market areas.*** Sales to specialized markets were increasing rapidly, with new attention being directed to supermarket, drugstore and grocery store chains; products being moved into mass merchandise promotions and educational catalogs, direct sales to corporate entities, onto the internet, etc.

8. ***Bookstores carrying more non-book items***. Increasing shelf space in the bookstores was being devoted to audio tapes, video tapes, cards, games, toys, magazines, stuffed animals, and other novelty and odds-and-ends impulse items.

9. ***More new titles being produced than the industry could absorb***. The quantity of available titles was increasing more rapidly than the amount of shelf and rack space to display them. This put increased pressure on publishers to take extraordinary actions to turn their inventories. More than one individual interviewed spoke of a "glut on the market" which would lead to the "inevitable shake out."

10. ***Booksellers buying more selectively***. More bookstores seemed to be looking for the "big books" and "big authors" and passing over many titles which they would have purchased previously. Some respondents felt the booksellers were buying fewer titles. This was causing more competition for publishers in their efforts to market mid-list books, and it was compelling them to meet the increasing challenge to promote their books more effectively.

11. ***Telemarketing expanding and being better accepted***. Stores appeared to be more willing to deal with telephone sales representatives than they were several years previously.

12. ***Book prices increasing***. Several large increases in the price of paper early in 1988 and following years significantly influenced the price of new books. This was especially visible with mass market paperbacks. The processing of more books through distributors and outside sales reps also contributed to increased book prices.

13. ***Trade paperbacks increasing***. A larger percentage of books was being produced in trade paperback format. The trade paperback area was regarded as healthy, with the books enjoying increasingly long back-list life. There was more competition in this area, and the cost of trade paperback reprint rights for books previously released as hardbacks was increasing.

14. ***Industry management skills improving***. The publishers saw a significant increase in the operational abilities of 1988's typical bookstore manager and buyer. They reported the retail bookstore industry to be significantly more adept in its approach to the business environment than it was several years previously.

15. ***More consumers reading***. Though competition with television and other recreational activities was intense, there was a general perception among the surveyed publishers that more of the general public was returning to reading, and that more members of the older generation were emphasizing the importance of acquiring strong reading skills to their children.

TRENDS IN 1998

A decade after the trends previously listed in this chapter were noted, it is interesting to recognize that almost all of them are still taking place. But other things have changed, and this section will comment briefly on several of them.

1. ***Anti-trust lawsuits are being launched against large chain stores receiving preferential treatment***.

The American Booksellers Association, in league with 25 independent bookstores, filed an anti-trust lawsuit against the two largest bookstore chains: Barnes and Noble and Borders, asserting that they are using their clout with publishers to receive preferential treatment and to make secret illegal deals. They assert that the special deals and discounts the chains are getting from publishers are not available to independent bookstores, no matter how many books they buy.

The lawsuit is based on provisions of the Robinson-Patman Act, which bars inequitable terms of sale, and also on a California act designed to prohibit chains from receiving unearned discounts that can injure smaller competitors. The complaint listed these alleged illegal preferences given to the chains: (1) extra discounts, including off-schedule ones; (2) shared markdowns; (3) extra discounts on small orders, which are unavailable to smaller stores; (4) special terms for new stores or expansions; (5) special discounts for non-returnable purchases; (6) co-op advertising terms not available to independents; (7) the chains received co-op payments in excess of the advertising done; and (8) the chains fail to comply with co-op terms in ways demanded of independents.

Commentators observe that "the issue is one of economic power," stating "the two chains between them do $5 billion in annual business, which is more than the 10 biggest publishers combined."

Publishers have complained of strong-arm tactics on the part of major chains saying, "We're scared of them. If they don't like our terms of sale they threaten not to buy our books."

The lawsuit is a pivotal case which can change the entire face of book selling for years to come. If the ABA and independent booksellers win, they can effectively curtail the excessive discounts the chains have used to pull business away from the independent bookstores (*Publishers Weekly*, 3/23/98, p. 16).

2. ***Major chains file for chapter 11 protection.***

Lauriat's is one of the largest, if not *the* largest, bookstore operation ever to file for bankruptcy protection. Though it had 1997 sales of approximately $120 million, and has more than a thousand employees, Lauriat's had total liabilities of $82.1 million, with assets of only $60.6 million at the end of 1997. It has approximately 5,000 creditors, to which it owes $43.4 million; $19 million of that total is owed to its 20 largest creditors, including Random House ($4.7 million), Bantam Doubleday Dell ($2.2 million), and Simon & Schuster ($1.9 million). It's apparently another case of unprofitable excessive chain-store discounting (*Publishers Weekly*, 3/9/98, p. 10).

Other chains have also sought for bankruptcy protection in recent months. In particular, regional chains have been hard hit. Recent bankruptcies include Crown Books, the Gaylord Companies (which operated five Little Professor Bookstores in Ohio), Village Green Bookstores (12 stores in upstate New York), Honolulu Book Shops (5 stores in Hawaii). Other notable bankruptcies during the 1990s include Media Play, Taylors (in Dallas), Kroch's and Brentano's (Chicago), Oxford Books (Atlanta), and Booksellers Cleveland (Cleveland) (*Publishers Weekly*, 8/3/98, pp. 49-50).

3. ***Big chain outlets have horrendous return rates.***

Reviews of 1996 industry trends focused so forcefully on unacceptable and out-of-control return rates that reducing large chain-store returns became the number one objective for 1997. Barnes and Noble's 1996 average return rate for *all categories of books* was 28%; that return rate for all categories of books was dropped to 19% in 1997. But Barnes and Noble's average rate on *new adult trade hardcovers* in 1997 was still an extremely high 36.7%—regarded by everyone as an unacceptable level (*Publishers Weekly*, 3/23/98, p. 41).

4. ***Sales are down in adult trade hardcover books.***

Overall sales of adult trade hardcover books were down 6.8% in 1997 from 1996 sales. This was perceived to be the result of the large chains attempting to get their just-in-time ordering programs under control and of their striving to reduce their extremely large return levels (*Publishers Weekly*, 3/28/98, p. 41).

5. ***Numerous celebrity books with large advances failed to reach earn-out sales levels in 1997.***

So many celebrity books released in 1997 failed to yield as much as was paid in advances to the authors that the lead article in *Publishers Weekly's* 1997 report was subtitled "a look at some of the major adult trade disappointments." The year was regarded as the year of the "adult trade hardcover correction," with a landslide of such problem reports as "its timing was off," they had to use "shared markdowns to get rid of stock," "this didn't successfully cross over to the New Age market," the book had "a too subtle cover," "only a 15% sell-through," "it failed to connect to an audience," "the cautious marketplace," "poor publicity support," and the publisher was "allowing books to die on the vine." Other complaints/excuses were: "the cover of the book was problematic. It was subtle; it didn't read 'blockbuster'," "a key problem was the lack of full tour and media for this book," "we erroneously thought he was a brand name," "the title and cover for the book didn't convey the message," etc. The year was regarded in the summary book article as a "pack of celebrity book bombs," as also were many of 1996's high-advance celebrity books, with the result that "celebrity book advances got closer across-the-board scrutiny last year." Thus the year was regarded as the year of the "big book correction" (*Publishers Weekly*, 3/23/98, pp. 41-49).

6. ***Many bookstores are selling vigorously on the Internet***. *Amazon.com* was joined by *BarnesandNoble.com*, Oregon-based *altbookstore.com*, Canadian-based *chapters-globe.com*, and a host of other major bookstore sites in selling on the Internet. The problem: "many sites are offering "discounts of 20% to 40%." This is bringing the complaint that "the discount price point they have set online is negative. Real-world bookstores can't compete. . . .Their model for market penetration is harmful to the industry." This observation is born out by reports that both *amazon.com* and *Barnesand Noble.com*, with their many millions of dollars in sales, have yet to operate in the black after several years of operation and annual multi-million dollar losses.

Yet optimism for Internet sales growth abounds. For instance, a representative from *Chapters*, the Canadian outlet mentioned above, said of their web sales volume (currently accounting for 1-2% of their sales), "forecasters predict Web sales could eventually account for 15% of Canadian retail book sales" (*Publishers Weekly,* 3/13/98, p. 18; 4/6/98, p. 10).

7. ***Many publishers are selling retail on the Internet.***

Publishers Weekly reports that "Small presses are everywhere on the Internet, and they're using the medium for everything from building a community to selling their books—often internationally." Various publishers report that "Our site allows us substantial contact with readers that we wouldn't otherwise have," that "the real power is exposure internationally," and that "many of the online orders are coming from outside the U.S" (*Publishers Weekly* suggests that for an extensive listing of Publishers on the Web, you may wish to visit the BookWire index at *www.bookwire.com/index/publishers.html.*) (*Publishers Weekly*, 3/23/98, pp. 34-35).

8. ***Territorial publishing rights are being eroded as Internet sales go world-wide.***

The ability of individuals across the world to order books through the Internet is reducing the sale of territorial rights in the United Kingdom, Europe, Australia, and other areas. There seems to be little incentive to police territorial rights, and crossovers have become increasingly common. United Kingdom observers have predicted that "in five years, the U.K. will become an export market and cease to be a licensing market," and that "in 2010 there will not be any territorial integrities" (*Publishers Weekly*, 6/29/98, p. 18).

9. ***Bookstore "territories" are ceasing to exist.***

With easy access to the Internet, and with the expansion of book-club and mail-order sales across the nation, the time is almost past when a bookstore can assert that a particular geographical area is its private territory. More than ever, bookstores are having to compete with good service and selection, and with careful attention to meeting the needs of their clientele. If new customers are not treated well, they will go elsewhere for the books they wish to purchase.

10. ***"On demand" electronic publishing is making its debut.***

On-demand electronic publishing, in which a previously typeset book is scanned into a computer and then a single copy or a very short print run is reproduced, is becoming a significant movement in the educational marketplace. This technology is providing a convenient way to satisfy the need for out-of-print and backlist titles, and is an excellent source of supply for students needing textbooks. This phenomenon is known as the "electronic retail revolution," or "on-demand printing," and has been made possible through the recent advances in computer technology and the linking of that technology with new developments in the printing industry such as DocuTech and similar Print on Demand (POD) printing systems (*Publishers Weekly*, 6/8/98, p. 29; 6/22/98, pp. 64-65).

11. ***Large, publicly traded companies are influencing the publishing business.***

At a recent convention, the book review editor for the *Los Angeles Times* stated that "serious trade book publishing is undergoing its most serious structural crisis in 100 years." Another speaker made reference to "the financial trouble we all find ourselves in," and said that the problem lay with the expectations of the publicly traded companies that had bought the large publishing houses in the "false hope of seeing double-digit growth," and observed emphatically that "that is unrealistic." He predicted that "the next cycle of significant expansion would be among independent publishers, which would grow in size from the $30-million to $50-million range to the $300-million range over the next decade, sparking a new round of consolidatio." (*Publishers Weekly*, 5/4/98, p. 20).

12. ***Small publishers are surviving through careful management and niche publishing.***

"The climate is changing in trade publishing, with staffs, advances and lists all being cut," says one small publisher's spokesman. Small publishers are hanging in with careful managing, maintenance of strong backlists, concentrating on rights sales, and making short print runs profitable through careful management. Another small publisher noted that "with their large overheads, major publishers now have to do a minimum first run of 20,000-30,000 copies. For a smaller publisher, a title selling 5,000-10,000 copies is very profitable."

Last year, Barnes and Noble reported that books from the 10 leading publishers accounted for less than half their purchases in the third quarter. Three years earlier, purchases from those publishers accounted for three-quarters of their purchases.

As they chart their own course, small publishers note that "More than ever, small publishers have to leverage the strengths we have and publish credible books for our readers. We've got to set our own courses and work both traditional marketing channels as well as new ones" (*Publishers Weekly*, 6/15/98, p. 35).

13. ***Middle-aged Baby Boomers are shaping the marketplace.***

"That thundering roar in the distance is, of course, baby boomers stampeding in droves toward their mid-century marks. Just as this set has impacted pop culture throughout their lives, boomers are now prompting publishers to come up with titles about aging." They're also responsible for the emphasis on books about all aspects of spirituality, books on parent-child relationships and parental love, books on acquiring new knowledge, and strong interest in books on angels and the many aspects of life after death (*Publishers Weekly*, 4/20/98, pp. 31-33).

14. ***Demand for New Age books continues to be strong.***

There's less dispute about what is a new-age book now, since the term has become so broad that "it encompasses the search for wisdom, love, happiness, harmony, balance, simplicity, and spirituality in all its forms." "No one predicts anything but continued growth for a long time to come for this genre of books as the American imagination is energized by deep encounters of the spiritual kind. People are hungry for angels, spirits and the understanding that comes from being in touch with a deeper dimension."

Booksellers have found that "In religion and spirituality, people are looking to traditional roots, but they are also showing a willingness to stretch the limits of their belief."

It appears that New Age is becoming so thoroughly integrated into the cultural mainstream that many different publishers are bringing out books that fall into this expanded genre. Though there is more competition at every stage of the process, there's still room for growth in this exciting publishing area. (*Publishers Weekly*, 4/13/98, pp. 30-35)

15. ***Religion sales are up significantly.***

Over the past five years, the religion/spirituality category has commanded unprecedented attention on the trade-show circuit. In addition to the Christian Bookseller sales conventions, BookExpo America (the new name for the American Booksellers convention) has increased its attention to religion, allocating more than 12,000 square feet to religious publishers and noting that approximately 10% of the attendees to their last convention were religion retailers.

Many other smaller trade shows are now being organized which focus on religious titles, including the Religious Booksellers Trade Exhibit (RBTE), the International New Age Trade Show (INATS), the ECPA regional shows, the CBA Expo, the Catholic Marketing Network (CMN), and the LDS Booksellers Association. (*Publishers Weekly*, 5/25/98, p. 54)

Ingram Book Company reported that its religion sales were up 58% during the first quarter of 1998, and that they did $9.2 million in sales in the religion category during 1997. (*Publishers Weekly*, 6/22/98, p. 66)

13

The State of the Industry: An Analysis of 1997 Sales

This chapter is a brief summation of the status of the book publishing and book selling industries as of December 31, 1997. It is based on data provided through articles in *Publishers Weekly*, and the reader is referred to those articles for more in-depth information.

BOOKSTORE SALES

U.S. Census Bureau preliminary estimates for the year 1997 show that bookstore sales during the year totaled $11.82 billion. This was an increase of 2.4% over 1996 sales, but it was approximately 27% less than the 3.3% gain of U.S. retail sales in general.

Unexpectedly soft consumer sales were largely responsible for the 1997 overall sales being less than half of the 5.3% increase projected for the year 1997 by the Book Industry Study Group. Unit sales actually declined 3.4% during 1997. Sales in the adult segment have not increased since 1994.

Mass market paperback 1997 sales fell 7.8% below their sales in 1996.

The bookstore sales were strengthened by better-than-expected sales in November and December. November sales increased 4.8% to $912 million; December sales were $1.63 billion, which was a 6.5% increase over December 1996 sales. (*Publishers Weekly*, 3/23/98, p. 19; 7/27/98, p. 8)

THE CONSUMER RESEARCH STUDY ON BOOK PURCHASING

A consumer research study, *The 1997 Consumer Research Study on Book Purchasing*, was prepared by the NPD Group and was summarized in the *Publishers Weekly* on June 8, 1998, p. 12. Here are the key findings of the report:

Sales by Outlet Type

1. The number of adult books purchased by consumers rose by less than 1% in 1997, with 1.07 billion units purchased. The report noted that with a 1% general population increase during 1997, consumers purchased fewer books on a per-household basis during the year than they did in 1996.

2. Bookstore chains and independent booksellers still accounted for the largest percentage of books purchased. They

sold 42% of total sales, a decline of 1% from 1996. The large chains sold 25% of the books sold to adults, while the market share of the independents and small chains fell from 24% in 1993, to 18% in 1996, to 17% in 1997. The 1% drop from 1996 represented a 7% decline in unit sales. (1996 had shown a 1.9% decline in their unit sales.)

3. Book clubs had a 20% market share in 1997, an increase from 16% in 1993. This was the first year more books were acquired through book clubs than through the combined sales of the independents and small chains.

4. Books bought through warehouse clubs and mass merchandisers held steady at 6% each during 1997, while sales through other discount outlets held at 3%.

5. The mail-order book marketing segment increased 1%, to 6% of total sales. This category now includes book sales made through the Internet, although Internet sales in 1997 accounted for only 0.3% of total book sales.

6. Multiple-media stores, which sell books along with a variety of other media products, accounted for 1% of total book sales in 1997.

7. Foodstore and drugstore book sales fell from 5% to 4% of total book sales in 1997.

8. Used book outlets' book sales fell from 4% to 3% for the year.

9. All other channels combined maintained their 9% market share for 1997.

Sales by Type of Book

1. Unit sales of children's books fell to 519 million in 1997, from 535 million in 1996 (a 3% drop).

2. Sales of paperbacks continued to erode in 1997, though still accounting for 59% of all book purchases. The paperback share was down from 60% in 1996, and 63% in 1993.

3. Hardcovers increased their share from 37% in 1996 to 38% in 1997. The remaining 3% of units sold were boxed sets.

4. There was a decline in the number of books purchased as gifts.

5. There was a decline in the number of books purchased by the heaviest book buyers.

6. While book sales over the Internet were slow in 1997, it appears that consumers now have accepted the Internet as a way of making book purchases.

7. Given the strong general economy and the weak performance by the book industry, it appears that the book market is a counter-cyclical business. (*Publishers Weekly*, 6/8/98, p. 12)

Outlet Share of Adult Book Purchasing, 1997

Large Chain Bookstores	25%
Book Clubs	20%
Independent/Small Chain Bookstores	17%
All Other Outlets	9%
Mail Order	6%
Mass Merchandisers	6%
Warehouse Clubs	6%
Food/Drug Stores	4%
Other Discount Stores	3%
Used Books	3%
Multi-Media	1%

ADDITIONAL PERSPECTIVES ON 1997 SALES

Another study, based on preliminary estimates released by the Association of American Publishers in March, 1998, gave these added insights on sales during the 1997 year:

1. Total book sales increased 2.4% to $21.28 billion. The increase was below the 4.2% gain registered in 1996, and was significantly less than the 4.7% compounded annual growth rate maintained between 1992 and 1997.

2. The best performers during 1997 were the educational publishing segments. Sales in the elementary-high school category rose 13%, to $2.96 billion. Sales in the higher-education segment rose 7.4% to $2.67 billion. These sectors have benefited from strong local economies and solid college enrollments. The standardized test segment saw sales increase 7.1% to $191.4 million. These three combined segments were the best performers in the industry during the 1997 year.

3. Sales in the trade segment were a major disappointment. Total trade sales fell 3.4% in 1997 to $5.45 billion.

4. Adult hardcover sales declined 6.8% during the year to $2.41 billion. This was the third year sales of adult hardcover books had fallen, and they are now down 9% since 1995.

5. Children's paperback sales fell by 18.9% to $470.3 million, probably caused, in the main, by a decline in the sales of *Goosebumps*.

6. Sales in the trade paperback segment rose 4.7%, to $1.68 billion.

7. Children's hardcovers increased 2.3% to $887.7 million.

8. Mass market paperbacks declined in sales 7.8% to $1.43 billion.

9. Mail-order sales fell 10.1% to $521 million.

10. Bible sales fell during the year, though an increase in the sales of other religious books yielded a 3.6% increase for the religious book segment, to $1.13 billion.

11. Sales of professional books increased 4.3%, to $4.16 billion.

12. Sales through book clubs increased 4.9% to $1.14 billion. During the past five years, the book-club segment has posted the highest annual growth rate, at 9.1%.

13. Sales at university presses increased 5.3% to $367.8 million.

14. Sales of subscription reference works rose 4.3%. (*Publishers Weekly*, 3/2/98, p. 11)

Preliminary Estimated Book Sales
1996-1997 ($ in millions)

Segment	1996	1997	% change
Trade	$5,643.0	$5,453.0	-3.4%
Adult hardcover	2,586.0	2,410.2	-6.8
Adult paperback	1,609.4	1,685.0	4.7
Juvenile hardcover	867.7	887.7	2.3
Juvenile paperback	579.9	470.3	-18.6
Religious	1,093.4	1,132.7	3.6

Bibles	294.8	285.4	-3.2
Other religious	798.6	847.3	6.1

Segment	**1996**	**1997**	**% change**
Professional	3,985.0	4,156.4	4.3
Book clubs	1,091.8	1,145.3	4.9
Mail order	579.5	521.0	-10.1
Mass market paperback	1,555.1	1,433.8	-7.8
University presses	349.3	367.8	5.3
Elementary-high school	2,619.1	2,959.6	13.0
Higher education	2,485.8	2,669.7	7.4
Standardized tests	178.7	191.4	7.1
Subscription reference	706.1	736.5	4.3
Other	493.2	510.0	3.4
Totals	**20,780.0**	**21,277.4**	**2.4**

(*Publishers Weekly*, 3/23/98, p. 17.)

SALES OF CHILDREN'S BOOKS

The following two charts give a clear indication of how children's books were sold in 1997 and what types of books were purchased. The third chart shows children's books sold by year, over the last decade, in millions of dollars and millions of units, with projections for 1998 included. (*Publishers Weekly*, 7/20/98, p. 121.)

Children's Books Sold in the U.S., by Outlet

1997

Book Clubs	19%
Mass Merchandisers	18%
All others	15%
Other discount stores	13%
Food/drug stores	8%
Independent/small chain bookstores	8%
Large chain bookstores	7%
Mail order	6%
Toy stores	4%
Warehouse/price clubs	2%
	100%

Types of Children's Books Purchased, 1997

Fiction & picture books	46%
Coloring & activity books	27%
Nonfiction	11%
Educational	6%
Religious.	5%
Book & tape	2%
Electronic	2%
Reference	1%
	100%

Children's Books Sold, by Year

Year	Dollars	Year	Units
1987	635,100,000	1987	726,700,000
1988	751,200,000	1988	262,100,000
1989	901,500,000	1989	289,600,000
1990	1,021,100,000	1990	310,300,000
1991	1,163,800,000	1991	335,000,000
1992	1,177,400,000	1992	327,900,000
1993	1,136,100,000	1993	307,400,000
1994	1,216,400,000	1994	329,000,000
1995	1,326,700,000	1995	357,100,000
1996	1,447,600,000	1996	379,900,000
1997	1,358,000,000	1997	343,600,000
1998*	1,437,600,000	1998*	355,900,000

**Book Industry Study Group* Projection

BOOK SALES PROJECTIONS FOR 1998

Though 1997's sales increase of 2.4% was less than half of the Book Industry Study Group's 5.3% 1997 projection, that group is projecting a rosy 4.4% increase for 1998.

The following are their estimates, by segment:

1. Consumer sales: 0.8% increase.
2. College sales: 6.9% increase, to $2.85 billion.
3. School sales: 4.8% increase.
4. Professional sales: 6% increase, to $4.40 billion.
5. Juvenile sales: 5.9% increase, to just under 1996 levels.

6. Adult sales: 1.6% increase, to $4.16 billion ($35 million below 1996).
7. Mass market sales: 3.2% increase.
8. Book club sales: 5.4% increase (following a 4.9% increase in 1997).
9. Mail order sales: 3.1% decrease.
10. Religious sales: 4% increase, to $1.18 billion.
11. University sales: 3.9% increase.

The following chart summarizes the publishers' projected sales for 1998, comparing them to actual 1997 sales. (*Publishers Weekly*, 7/27/98, p. 8.)

Publishers' Projected Sales, 1998, in Dollars and Units (in millions)

	1997		1998		% Change	
Segment	**Units**	**$**	**Units**	**$**	**Units**	**$**
Adult	441.8	$4,095.2	438.9	$4,160.0	-0.7%	1.6%
Juvenile	343.8	1,358.0	355.9	1,437.6	3.5	5.9
Mass Market	473.2	1,433.8	472.3	1,480.3	-0.2	3.2
Book Clubs	137.7	1,145.3	141.3	1,207.2	2.6	5.4
Mail Order	85.7	521.0	81.8	504.7	-4.6	-3.1
Religious	166.6	1,132.7	170.3	1,178.0	2.2	4.0
Professional	165.2	4,156.4	169.6	4,404.6	2.6	6.0
University Press	17.8	367.8	18.0	382.1	1.0	3.9
Elem.–High School	286.5	2,959.6	282.8	3,102.4	-1.3	4.8
College	168.2	2,669.7	173.7	2,852.8	3.2	6.9
Standardized Tests	—	191.4	—	204.3	—	6.8
Subject Reference	1.2	736.5	1.2	766.9	0.1	4.1
Totals	**2,287.7**	**20,767.4**	**2,305.8**	**21,680.9**	**0.8**	**4.4**

CHAIN STORE SALES

Total sales for the nation's four largest bookstore chains rose 14.3%, to $5.68 billion dollars, for the fiscal year which ended January 31, 1998. The 14.3% gain was less than their 17.3% gain for 1996, but substantially larger than the 2.4% increase for overall bookstore sales. Obviously, these major chains have siphoned off a large share of the bookstore marketplace from the independent bookstores and small chains.

The following chart reflects total 1997 sales and 1998 projections for the four largest bookstore chain operations:

Barnes & Noble, Borders Group, Books-A-Million, and Crown Books. (*Publishers Weekly*, 3/23/98, p. 17)

Quarterly Bookstore Chain Sales (in millions)

Chain	1998	1997	% change
Full Year			
Barnes & Noble	$2,797.0	$2,448.0	14.2%
Borders Group	2,266.0	1,958.8	15.7
Books-A-Million	324.8	278.6	16.5
Crown Books	297.5	287.7	3.4
Totals	**$5,685.3**	**$4,973.1**	**14.3%**
Fourth Quarter			
Barnes & Noble	$968.5	$882.5	9.7%
Borders Group	858.8	727.0	13.1
Books-A-Million	113.0	97.0	16.5
Crown Books	98.3	95.4	3.0
Totals	**$2,038.6**	**$1,801.9**	**13.1%**

PUBLICLY TRADED PUBLISHING COMPANIES

Profitability increased for 11 of the 17 major publicly traded book publishers during 1997. This was an improvement over 1996, when only nine of the 17 improved their bottom lines, and over 1995, when only five of the 17 increased their profit margins.

The following chart compares their 1996 and 1997 revenues, operating incomes, and profit margins.
(*Publishers Weekly*, 8/10/98, p. 232)

Operating Performance of Publicly Held Book Publishers, 1996-97 ($ in millions)

	1996 Operating Data			1997 Operating Data		
	Revenue	Operating Income	Margin	Revenue	Operating Income	Margin
Dove	$26.8	($6.4)	-23.8%	$16.7	($16.0)	-95.8%
EDC	21.2	1.6	7.5	19.3	1.7	8.8
Golden Books	255.0	(195.6)	-76.7	243.5	(49.6)	-20.3

Harcourt Brace*	1092.6	197.0	18.0	1376.3	(139.0)	-10.0
Harlequin*	C$509.3	C$81.0	15.9	C$489.7	C$81.3	16.6
HarperCollins*[1]	932.0	68.0	7.3	737.0	12.0	1.6
Houghton Mifflin	717.9	87.4	12.1	797.3	106.5	13.3
IDG Books[2]	97.8	11.0	11.2	120.7	11.9	9.8
McGraw-Hill Ed.*	1277.9	151.9	9.0	1573.8	187.7	11.9
Pearson*[3]	£934.5	£99.1	10.6	£1088.4	£117.4	10.8
Reader's Digest*[4]	2100.0	322.1	15.3	1850.5	201.1	10.9
Scholastic[5]	966.3	17.7	1.8	1058.7	48.1	4.5
Simon & Schuster*	2331.7	217.2	9.3	2472.1	221.7	9.0
Thomas Nelson[6]	243.4	9.5	3.9	253.0	12.7	5.0
Times Mirror*[7]	1031.2	58.7	5.7	852.9	143.4	16.8
Waverly	171.0	6.3	3.7	172.4	7.1	4.1
John Wiley[8]	432.0	34.8	8.0	467.1	45.3	9.7

(1) For fiscal years ended June 30, 1997, 1996. (2) For fiscal years ended Sept. 31, 1997, 1996. (3) Combination of Penguin Putnam and AWL. (4) For book publishing & video units for fiscal years ended June 30, 1997, 1996. (5) For fiscal years ended May 31, 1998, 1997. (6) For fiscal years ended March 31, 1998, 1997. (7) Professional Information Group. (8) For fiscal years ended April 30, 1998, 1997. *Denotes companies where corporate expenses are not deducted prior to operating income.

Publishers Weekly also tracks the stock performances of the publicly traded publishing corporations on a monthly basis. The following is a typical monthly listing, reflecting the stocks' status at the beginning and end of April 1998:

Publisher Stocks: April 1998 Performances

Company	March 31	April 30	% change
Winners			
Crown Books	$6\frac{13}{16}$	$7\frac{3}{4}$	14.0%
Time Warner	72	$78\frac{1}{2}$	9.0
Donnelley	$40\frac{1}{2}$	$44\frac{1}{16}$	8.8
Viacom	$53\frac{1}{8}$	$57\frac{3}{4}$	8.7
Amazon.com	$85\frac{17}{32}$	$91\frac{3}{4}$	7.3
Losers			
Barnes & Noble	39	$33\frac{7}{8}$	-13.1
Scholastic	$42\frac{1}{4}$	$37\frac{1}{4}$	-11.8
Tribune Co.	$70\frac{1}{2}$	66	-6.4
Harcourt General	$55\frac{3}{8}$	$52\frac{3}{16}$	-5.7
Borders Group	$34\frac{1}{16}$	$32\frac{1}{84}$	-5.7

Publishers Weekly

Stock Index	866.03	870.15	0.4%
Dow Jones Average	8799.81	9063.37	3.0%

(*Publishers Weekly*, 5/11/98, p. 14.)

HARDBOUND FICTION BEST-SELLERS

1997 was the first year ever that the number of novels produced in hardback editions reached three digits—exactly 100 sold at that level. The previous record, tied in 1995 and 1996, was 93 titles. The quantities sold are listed in the March 23, 1998 issue of *Publishers Weekly*, pp. 50-55. Rankings are based on sales figures provided by the publishers, and generally reflect the number of copies "billed and shipped" during calendar year 1997, less returns which they had received through February 10, 1998. Since the majority of returns typically occur after that date, none of the figures listed can be considered as final net sales. Some publishers provided sales figures in confidence, which allowed the books to be ranked. For the purpose of sorting titles by total number sold, this database has showed the total sales number for books listed without the quantity sold to be one book more than the total for the book just below it.

1997 Hardbound Fiction Best-Sellers

Author	Title	Publisher	Sold
THE TOP 30			
1 Grisham, John	The Partner	Doubleday	2,625,000
2 Frazier, Charles	Cold Mountain	Atlantic Monthly	1,458,280
3 Steel, Danielle	The Ghost	Delacorte	1,161,121
4 Steel, Danielle	The Ranch	Delacorte	1,158,631
5 Steel, Danielle	Special Delivery	Delacorte	1,152,937
6 Corwell, Patricia	Unnatural Exposure	Putnam	869,682
7 Sheldon, Sidney	The Best Laid Plans	Morrow	730,755
8 Clark, Mary Higgins	Pretend You Don't See Her	Simon & Schuster	750,000
9 Patterson, James	Cat & Mouse	Little, Brown	701,237
10 Corwell, Patricia	Hornet's Nest	Putnam	636,400
11 Evans, Richard Paul	The Letter	Simon & Schuster	575,000
12 Cussler, Clive	Flood Tide	Simon & Schuster	550,000
13 Rice, Anne	Violin	Knopf	501,702
14 Ludlum, Robert	The Matarese Countdown	Bantam	500,000
15 DeMille, Nelson	Plum Island	Warner	474,848
16 Baldacci, David	The Winner	Warner	433,648
17 Spencer, LaVyrle	Then Came Heaven	Putnam	349,671

18	Carr, Caleb	The Angel of Darkness	Random House	438,335
19	Brown, Sandra	Fat Tuesday	Warner	339,089
20	Spencer, LaVyrle	Small Town Girl	Putnam	331,550
21	Kellerman, Jonathan	Survival of the Fittest	Bantam	324,709
	Author	**Title**	**Publisher**	**Sold**
22	Binchy, Maeve	This Year It Will be Different	Delacorte	324,708
23	Dunne, Dominick	Another City, Not My Own	Crown	313,367
24	Garwood, Julie	Come the Spring	Pocket	311,282
25	Cook, Robin	Chromosome 6	Putnam	311,281
26	McMurtry, Larry	Comanche Moon	Simon & Schuster	300,589
27	Sparks, Nicholas	The Notebook	Warner	300,597
28	Koontz, Dean	Sole Survivor	Knopf	299,615
29	DeLillo, Don	Underworld	Scribner	290,000
30	Francis, Dick	10 Lb. Penalty	Putnam	275,794
		200,000+ TITLES		
31	Roberts, Nora	Sanctuary	Putnam	200,000+
32	Sanford, John	Night Crew	Putnam	200,000+
33	Martini, Steve	The List	Putnam	200,000+
34	Clarke, Arthur C.	The Final Odyssey	Del Rey	200,000+
35	Keillor, Garrison	Wobegon Boy	Viking	200,000+
36	Lindsey, Johanna	All I Need Is You	Avon	200,000+
37	Patterson, Richard North	Silent Witness	Knopf	200,000+
38	Binchy, Maeve	Evening Class	Delacorte	200,000+
39	Roy, Arundhati	The God of Small Things	Random House	200,000+
40	Brown, Sandra	Tidings of Great Joy	Bantam	200,000+
41	Higgins, Jack	The President's Daughter	Putnam	200,000+
42	Sanders, Lawrence	McNally's Gamble	Putnam	200,000+
43	Reichs, Kathy	Deja Dead	Scribner	200,000+
44	Kellerman, Jonathan	The Clinic	Bantam	200,000+
45	Gabaldon, Diana	Drums of Autumn	Delacorte	200,000+
46	Coulter, Catherine	The Maze	Putnam	200,000+
47	Plain, Belva	Homecoming	Delacorte	200,000+
48	Preston, Richard	The Cobra Event	Random House	200,000+
49	Higaasen, Carl	Lucky You	Random House	200,000+
50	Vonnegut, Kurt	Timequake	Putnam	200,000+
51	Braun, Lilian Jackson	The Cat Who Tailed a Thief	Putnam	200,000+
		150,000+ TITLES		
52	Rutherfurd, Edward	London	Crown	150,000+
53	Griffin, W.E.B.	The Last Heroes	Putnam	150,000+
54	James, P. D.	A Certain Justice	Knopf	150,000+
55	Beltzer, Brad	The Tenth Justice	Morrow/Rob Weisbach	150,000+
56	Harris, E. Lynn	If This World Were Mine	Doubleday	150,000+
57	Travolta, John	Propeller One-Way Night	Warner	150,000+
58	Kleier, Glenn	The Last Day	Warner	150,000+
59	Kellerman, Faye	Serpent's Tooth	Morrow	150,000+
60	Plain, Belva	Secrecy	Delacorte	150,000+
61	Carcaterra, Lorenzo	Apaches	Ballantine	150,000+
62	Holm, Ann, et al.	Upon a Midnight Clear	Pocket	150,000+

	Author	Title	Publisher	Sold
63	Hoag, Tami	A Thin Dark Line	Bantam	150,000+
64	Zahn, Timothy	Star Wars: Specter of the Past	Bantam	150,000+

	Author	Title	Publisher	Sold
		125,000+ TITLES		
65	Parker, Robert	Small Vices	Putnam	125,000+
66	George, Elizabeth	Deception on His Mind	Bantam	125,000+
67	Karon, Jan	Out to Canaan	Viking	125,000+
68	Parker, Robert	Night Passage	Putnam	125,000+
69	L'Amour, Louis	End of the Drive	Bantam	125,000+
70	Eddings, David & Leigh	Polgara the Sorceress	Del Rey	125,000+
71	Williamson, Martha	Touched by an Angel: A Christmas Miracle	Thomas Nelson	125,000+
72	Goodkind, Terry	Temple of the Winds	Tor	125,000+
73	Shatner, William	Star Trek: Avenger	Pocket	125,000+
74	Lucado, Max	Cosmic Christmas	Word	125,000+
75	Krentz, Jayne Ann	Deep Waters	Pocket	125,000+
76	Quick, Amanda	Affair	Bantam	125,000+
77	Brown, Dale	Fatal Terrain	Putnam	125,000+
78	Lowell, Elizabeth	Amber Beach	Avon	125,000+
79	Saul, John	The Presence	Fawcett	125,000+
		100,000+ TITLES		
80	Michael, Judith	Acts of Love	Crown	100,000+
81	Diehl, William	Reign in Hell	Ballantine	100,000+
82	Pynchon, Thomas	Mason & Dixon	Holt	100,000+
83	Brooks,Terry	Running with the Demon	Del Rey	100,000+
84	Golden, Arthur	Memoirs of a Geisha	Knopf	100,000+
85	Hamill, Pete	Snow in August	Little, Brown	100,000+
86	Mayle, Peter	Chasing Cezanne	Knopf	100,000+
87	McCaffrey, Anne	Dragonseve	Del Rey	100,000+
88	Roth, Philip	American Pastoral	Houghton Mifflin	100,000+
89	Silva, Daniel	The Unlikely Spy	Villard	100,000+
90	Delinsky, Barbara	Three Wishes	Simon & Schuster	100,000+
91	Gerritsen, Tess	Life Support	Pocket	100,000+
92	Heimerdinger, Chris	A Return to Christmas	Ballantine	100,000+
93	Braun, Lilian Jackson	The Cat Who Read Backwards	Putnam	100,000+
94	Case, John	The Genesis Code	Ballantine	100,000+
95	Segal, Erich	Only Love	Putnam	100,000+
96	Allen, Steve	Meg	Doubleday	100,000+
97	Jordan, Robert & Peterson, Teresa	Wheel of Time	Tor	100,000+
98	Brown, Sandra	Hawk O'Toole's Hostage	Bantam	100,000+
99	Hambly, Barbara	Star Wars: Planet of Twilight	Bantam	100,000+
100	Roberts, Nora	Public Secrets	Bantam	100,000+

HARDBOUND NON-FICTION BEST-SELLERS

A new record was set in 1997 for the number of non-fiction hardbound books which sold more than 100,000 copies: 127 books. This broke the record of 109 set in 1996.

1997 Hardbound Non-Fiction Best-Sellers

	Author	Title	Publisher	Sold
		THE TOP 30		
1	McCourt, Frank	Angela's Ashes	Scribner	1,650,000
2	Ban Breathnach, Sarah	Simple Abundance	Warner	1,462,663
3	Berendt, John	Midnight in the Garden of Good and Evil	Random House	1,300,799
4	Kelley, Kitty	The Royals	Warner	1,120,943
5	Rombauer, Irma S., et al.	Joy of Cooking	Scribner	1,000,000
6	Morton, Andrew	Diana: Her True Story	Simon & Schuster	825,000
7	Krakauer, Jon	Into Thin Air	Villard	784,969
8	Walsch, Neale Donald	Conversations with God, Bk. 1	Putnam	749,001
9	Gray, John	Men Are from Mars . . .	HarperCollins	687,267
10	Weil, Andrew	Eight Weeks to Optimum Health	Knopf	674,117
11	Graham, Billy	Just As I Am	Harper San Francisco/ Zondervan	647,008
12	Roberts, Monty	The Man Who Listens to Horses	Random House	593,165
13	Stanley, Thomas J. & Danko, William D.	The Millionaire Next Door	Longstreet	585,924
14	Junger, Sebastian	The Perfect Storm	Norton	550,000
15	O'Donnell, Rosie	Kids are Punny	Warner	558,880
16	Redfield, James	The Celestine Vision	Warner	551,656
17	Donnelly, Peter	Diana: A Tribute to the People's Princess	Courage	539,000
18	Clancy, Tom & Franks, Fred	Into the Storm	Putnam	527,017
19	Covey, Stephen R.	The 7 Habits of Highly Effective Families	Golden Books	505,000
20	Clark, Marcia with Carpenter, Teresa	Without a Doubt	Viking	502,605
21	Carlson, Richard	Don't Worry, Make Money	Hyperion	495,401
22	Theodosakis, Jason, et al.	The Arthritis Cure	St. Martin's	441,117
23	Drosnin, Michael	The Bible Code	Simon & Schuster	408,527
24	Hersh, Seymour	The Dark Side of Camelot	Little, Brown	408,526
25	Reiser, Paul	Babyhood	Morrow/Rob Weisbach	404,781
26	Carey, Drew	Dirty Jokes and Beer	Hyperion	396,292
27	Better Homes & Gardens (editors)	Better Homes & Gardens New Cook Book	Meredith	392,120
28	Goldberg, Whoopi	Book	Morrow/Rob Weisbach	367,156
29	Adams, Scott	The Dilbert Future	Harper Business	362,000
30	Mass, Peter	Underboss	HarperCollins	351,373

300,000+ TITLES

	Author	Title	Publisher	Sold
31	Walsch, Neale Donald	Conversations with God, Bk. 2	Hampton Roads	300,000+
32	Carlin, George	Brain Droppings	Hyperion	300,000+
33	Ambrose, Stephen	Citizen Soldiers	Simon & Schuster	300,000+
34	Bernardin, Joseph Cardinal	The Gift of Peace	Loyola University Press	300,000+
35	Albom, Mitch	Tuesdays With Morrie	Doubleday	300,000+
36	Better Homes & Gardens (editors)	Nestle Toll House Best Loved Cookies	Meredith	300,000+
37	Sears, Barry	The Zone	Regan Books	300,000+
38	D'Adams, Peter	Eat Right 4 Your Type	Putnam	300,000+
39	Somers, Suzanne	Suzanne Somers' Eat Great, Lose Weight	Crown	300,000+
40		The Merck Manual of Medical Information, Home Edition	Merck Research Laboratories	300,000+

200,000+ TITLES

	Author	Title	Publisher	Sold
41	Sears, Barry	Mastering the Zone	Regan Books	200,000+
42	Gray, John	Mars and Venus on a Date	HarperCollins	200,000+
43	Williamson, Marianne	Illuminated Prayers	Simon & Schuster	200,000+
44	Carter, Jimmy	Sources of Strength	Times Books	200,000+
45	Pitino, Rick	Success Is a Choice	Broadway	200,000+
46	deBecker, Gavin	The Gift of Fear	Little, Brown	200,000+
47	Schlessinger, Laura	10 Stupid Things Men Do to Mess Up Their Lives	HarperCollins	200,000+
48	O'Mara, Michael	Diana: A Tribute in Photographs	St. Martin's	200,000+
49	Woods, Earl	Training a Tiger	HarperCollins	200,000+
50	Goldman, Ron, et al.	His Name is Ron	Morrow	200,000+
51	Fuhrman, Mark	Murder in Brentwood	Regnery	200,000+
52	Saline, Carol & Wolmuth, Sharon	Mothers and Daughters	Doubleday	200,000+
53	Walsh, John with Schindehette, Susan	Tears of Rage	Pocket	200,000+
54	Angelon, Maya	Even the Stars Look Lonesome	Random House	200,000+
55	Graham, Katherine	Personal History	Knopf	200,000+
56	Stewart, Martha	Martha Stewart's Healthy Quick Cook	Clarkson Potter	200,000+
57	Orman, Suze	The Nine Steps to Financial Freedom	Crown	200,000+
58	Carper, Jean	Miracle Cures	HarperCollins	200,000+
59	Shamblin, Gwen	The Weigh Down Diet	Doubleday	200,000+
60	Goldschneider, Gary & Effers, Joost	The Secret Language of Relationships	Penguin Studio	200,000+
61	Cowen, Lauren	Daughters & Mothers	Courage	200,000+
62	Rimes, LeAnn & Carter, Tom	Holiday in Your Heart	Doubleday	200,000+
63	Lucado, Max	The Great House of God	Word	200,000+

	Author	Title	Publisher	Sold
64	Lange, Tom & Vannatter, Philip	Evidence Dismissed	Pocket	200,000+

	Author	Title	Publisher	Sold
65	Countryman, J. & Carlisle, Bob as told to Moldea, Don E.	Butterfly Kisses	Word	200,000+
66	Better Homes & Gardens (Editors)	Better Homes & Gardens 75 Years of All-Time Favorites	Meredith	200,000+

150,000+ TITLES

	Author	Title	Publisher	Sold
67	Aucoin, Kevin	Making Faces	Little, Brown	150,000+
68	Masson, Jeffrey M.	Dogs Never Lie About Love	Crown	150,000+
69	Goodwin, Doris Kearns	Wail Till Next Year	Simon & Schuster	150,000+
70	Rock, Chris	Rock This!	Hyperion	150,000+
71	Rodman, Dennis	Walk on the Wild Side	Delacorte	150,000+
72	Simmons, Richard	Sweetie Pie	GT Publishing	150,000+
73	Williamson, Marianne	The Healing of America	Simon & Schuster	150,000+
74	Harrer, Heinrich	Seven Years in Tibet	Putnam/Tarcher	150,000+
75	Nancy, Ted L.	Letters from a Nut	Avon	150,000+
76	Reese, Della	Angels Along the Way	Putnam	150,000+
77	Sears, Barry	Zone-Perfect Meals in Minutes	Regan Books	150,000+
78	Ripkin, Cal & Bryan, Mike	The Only Way I Know	Viking	150,000+
79	Ramsey, Dave	Financial Peace	Viking	150,000+
80	Peck, Richard	The Road Less Traveled and Beyond	Simon & Schuster	150,000+
81	Bennett, William J., ed.	Our Sacred Honor	Simon & Schuster	150,000+
82	Morgan, Lorrie	Forever Yours, Faithfully	Ballantine	150,000+
83	Better Homes & Gardens (Editors)	Better Homes and Gardens The New Decorating Book	Meredith	150,000+
84	Chopra, Deepak	The Seven Spiritual Laws for Parents	Harmony	150,000+
85	Lagasse, Emeril & Bienvenu, Marcelle	Emeril's Creole Christmas	Morrow	150,000+
86	Judd, Naomi	Naomi's Home Companion	GT Publishing	150,000+
87	Ingram, Julia & Hardin, G.W.	The Messengers	Pocket	150,000+

125,000+ TITLES

	Author	Title	Publisher	Sold
88	Oppenheimer, Jerry	Martha Stewart: Just Desserts	Morrow	125,000+
89	Countryman, J.	Joy for the Journey	Word	125,000+
90	Nelson, Miriam & Werneck, Sara	Strong Women Stay Young	Bantam	125,000+
91	Trump, Donald	Trump: The Art of the Comeback	Times Books	125,000+
92	St. James, Elaine	Simplify Your Life with Kids	Andrews McMeel	125,000+
93	Herriot, James	James Herriot's Animal Stories	St. Martin's	125,000+

	Author	Title	Publisher	Sold
94	Better Homes & Gardens (eds.)	Better Homes and Gardens Home Landscaping	Meredith	125,000+
95	Corso, Col. Philip (Ret.) & Burns, William	The Day After Roswell	Pocket	125,000+
96	Knight, Gladys	Between Each Line of Pain and Glory	Hyperion	125,000+
97	Fouveaux, Jessie Lee Brown	Any Given Day	Warner	125,000+
98	Levine, Kathy with Scovell, Jane	We Should Be So Lucky	Pocket	125,000+
99	Marcinko, Richard & Weisman, John	Rogue Warrior: Designation Gold	Pocket	125,000+
100	Vibe (eds.)	Tupac Shakur	Crown	125,000+
101	Spoto, Donald	Diana: The Last Year	Harmony	125,000+
102	Better Homes & Gardens (eds.)	Better Homes and Gardens New Dieter's Cookbook	Meredith	125,000+

100,000+ TITLES

	Author	Title	Publisher	Sold
103	Lunden, Joan & Morton, Laura	Joan Lunden's Healthy Living	Crown	100,000+
104	Pollan, Stephen	Die Broke	Harper/Business	100,000+
105	Love, Susan M. with Lindsay, Karen	Dr. Susan Love's Hormone Book	Random House	100,000+
106	Sedaris, David	Naked	Little, Brown	100,000+
107	Lucado, Max	In the Grip of Grace	Word	100,000+
108	Countryman, J. & Lucado, Max	God's Inspirational Promise	Word	100,000+
109	Fein, Ellen & & Schneider, Sherrie	Rules II	Warner	100,000+
110	Zehme, Bill	The Way You Wear Your Hat	HarperCollins	100,000+
111	Tucker, Tanya with Cox, Patsi Bale	Nickel Dreams	Hyperion	100,000+
112	Schultz, Howard with Yang, Dori Jones	Pour Your Heart into It	Hyperion	100,000+
113	Cowman, L.B., edited by Reimann, James	Streams in the Desert	Zondervan	100,000+
114	Hendrix, Harville & Hunt, Helen	Giving the Love That Heals	Pocket	100,000+
115	Beckwith, Harry	Selling the Invisible	Warner	100,000+
116	Swindoll, Charles R.	David: A Man of Passion & Destiny	Word	100,000+
117	Favre, Brett & Havel, Chris	Favre: Born on the Bayou, Bred for Greenbay	Doubleday	100,000+
118	Aerosmith with Davis, Stephen	Walk This Way: The Autobiography of Aerosmith	Avon	100,000+
119	Cool J, LL with Hunter, Karen	I Make My Own Rules	St. Martin's	100,000+
120	Barry, Dave	Dave Barry's Book	Andrews McMeel	100,000+

Author	Title	Publisher	Sold
	of Bad Songs		
121 Chaliha, Jaya & LeJoly, Edward, comp.	The Joy in Loving	Viking	100,000+
122 Sagan, Carl	Billions and Billions	Random House	100,000+
123 Murphy, Michael	The Kingdom of Shivas Irons	Broadway	100,000+
124 Mother Teresa	No Greater Love	New World Library	100,000+
125 McCord, Gary	Just a Rangeball in a Box of Titleists	Putnam	100,000+
126 DeVos, Dick	Rediscovering American Values	Dutton	100,000+
127 Hanegraaff, Hank	Counterfeit Revival	Word	100,000+

1997 TRADE PAPERBACK BEST-SELLERS

The list of trade paperback bestsellers primarily includes original or reprint editions published in 1996 or 1997. However, trade paperback books which had sales over 100,000 in 1997 which were published in earlier years have also been included, with the publication year indicated in parentheses in the Publisher column. (Source: *Publishers Weekly*, 3/23/98, pp. 56-64.)

1997 Trade Paperback Best-Sellers

	Author	Title	Publisher	Sold
		100,000+ TITLES		
1	Carlson, Richard	Don't Sweat the Small Stuff	Hyperion	4,506,683
2	Canfield, Jack; Hansen, Mark V. et al.	Chicken Soup for the Woman's Soul	Health Commun.	2,228,000
3	Lamb, Wally	She's Come Undone	Pocket/Wash. Sq.	1,406,740
4	Canfield, Jack; Hansen, Mark V. et al.	Chicken Soup for the Mother's Soul	Health Commun.	1,406,739
5	King, Stephen	Wizard and Glass	Plume	1,298,664
6	Hegi, Ursula	Stones from the River	Scribner	1,285,000
7	Balch, James E. & Phyllis A.	Rx for Nutritional Healing	Avery	1,275,000
8	Rathbone, Andy	Windows 95 for Dummies, 2nd ed.	IDG	1,148,107
9	Canfield, Jack; Hansen, Mark V. et al.	Chicken Soup for the Christian Soul	Health Commun.	1,263,328
10	Morris, Mary McGarry,	Songs in Ordinary Time	Penguin	1,120,000
11	Canfield, Jack; Hansen, Mark V. et al.	A 4th Course of Chicken Soup for the Soul	Health Commun.	1,088,952
12	Reynolds, Sheri	Rapture of Canaan	Berkley	1,000,000
23	Gaines, Ernest	A Lesson Before Dying	Vintage ('94)	901,298
24	Gibbons, Kaye	Ellen Foster	Vintage ('88)	775,303
25	Gibbons, Kaye	A Virtuous Woman	Vintage ('90)	698,215

	Author	Title	Publisher	Sold
13	Angelou, Maya	Heart of a Woman	Bantam	589,002
14	Woodiwiss, Kathleen E.	Petals on the River	Avon	589,001
15	Ambrose, Stephen E.	Undaunted Courage	Touchstone	589,000
16	Adams, Scott	Casual Day Has Gone Too Far	Andrews & McMeel	575,000
17	Weil, Andrew, M.D.	Spontaneous Healing	Fawcett	557,779
18	Krakauer, Jon	Into the Wild	Jon Krakauer	548,667
19	Levine, John	The Internet for Dummies	IDG	537,391
20	McBride, James	Color of Water	Riverhead	500,000
21	Adams, Scott	Seven Years of Highly Defective People	Andrews & McMeel	495,000
22	Balch, James E. & Phyllis A.	Prescription for Nutritional Healing	Avery	454,037
23	Harr, Jonathan	A Civil Action	Vintage	423,044
24	Canfield, Jack; Hansen, Mark V. et al.	Chicken Soup for the Soul at Work	Health Commun.	358,075
25	Gray, Alice	Stories for the Heart	Multnomah	357,111
26	Adams, Scott	The Dilbert Principle	Harper Business	300,000
37	Goleman, Daniel	Emotional Intelligence	Bantam	295,560
28	Wang, Wally	MS Office 97 for Windows for Dummies	IDG	295,559
29	Harvey, Gregory A.	Windows 95 for Dummies Quick Reference	IDG	285,673
30	Fowler, Connie May	Before Women Had Wings	Fawcett	276,646
31	France, Mayes	Under the Tuscan Sun: At Home in Italy	Broadway	274,919
32	Jenkins, Jerry & LaHaye, Tim	Left Behind	Tyndale	274,023
33	Steinbeck, Jyl	The Fat Free Living Super Cookbook	Warner	273,339
34	Redfield, James	The Celestine Prophecy	Warner	
35	Schlesinger, Laura	How Could You Do That	Haper Paperbacks	254,605
36	Karon, Jan	These High Green Hills	Penguin	250,000
36	Powter, Susan	Hey, Mom, I'm Hungry	Fireside	233,000
38		Teach Yourself Windows 95 Visually	Maragraphics	227,623
39	Jenkins, Jerry & LaHaye, Tim	Tribulation Force	Tyndale	225,263
40	Lukins, Sheila	USA Cookbook	Workman	221,286
41	Clancy, Tom	Airborne	Berkley	221,285
42	Allenbaugh, Kay	Chocolate for a Woman's Soul	Fireside	203,000
43	Harrer, Heinrich	Seven Years in Tibet	Tarcher	200,000
44	Johnson, Barbara	Living Somewhere Between Estrogen & Death	Word	196,471
45	Silvers, Robert	Photomosaics	Holt	186,001
46	Gardner, David & Tom	Motley Fool Investment Guide	Fireside	186,000
47	Hagee, John	Day of Deception	Thomas Nelson	185,198
48	Oke, Janette & Bunn, T. Davis	Another Homecoming	Bethany House	179,869

	Author	Title	Publisher	Sold
49	Adams, Scott	Dogbert's Top Secret Management Handbook	Harper Business	175,001
50	Atkins, Robert C. M.D. & Adkins, Veronica	Dr. Atkins Quick & Easy New Diet	Fireside	175,000
51	Cronkite, Walter	A Reporter's Life	Ballantine	174,466
52		The Illustrated Dream Dictionary	Sterling	172,394
53	Groening, Matt	The Simpsons: A Guide to Our Favorite Family	Harper Paperbacks	171,176
54	Sagan, Carl	The Demon-Haunted World	Ballantine	169,647
55	Gookin, Dan	PCs for Dummies, 4th ed.	IDG	165,319
56	Millhauser, Steven	Martin Dressler	Vintage	164,112
57	Norris, Kathleen	Cloister Walk	Riverhead	164,112
58	Rice, Anne	Servant of the Bones	Ballantine	162,003
59	Kaufeld, John	America Online for Dummies, 3rd ed.	IDG	159,152
60	Levine, John	The Internet for Dummies, Quick Reference, 3rd ed.	IDG	158,286
61	Peretti, Frank	The Oath	Word	156,286
62	Irons, Diane	The World's Best-Kept Beauty Secrets	Sourcebooks	155,934
63	Jamison, Kay	An Unquiet Mind	Vintage	154,848
64	Kushner, Harold	How Good Do We Have to Be?	Little, Brown	154,381
65	Tyson, Eric	Investing for Dummies	IDG	152,944
66	Canfield, Jack; Hansen, Mark V. et al.	A Cup of Chicken Soup for the Soul	Health Commun.	151,075
67	McCord, Gary	Golf for Dummies	IDG	150,944
68	Gookin, Dan	Word 97 for Windows for Dummies	IDG	150,055
69	Covey, Stephen R.	First Things First Everyday	Fireside	150,001
70	Walsh, Neal Donald	Meditations on Conversations w/ God	Berkley	150,000
71	Remen, Rachel	Kitchen Table Wisdom	Riverhead	149,817
72	Bombeck, Erma	Forever, Erma	Andrews & McMeel	147,000
73	Eds. of Better Homes & Gardens	Better Homes and Gardens New Cook Book	Meridith	145,538
74	Canfield, Jack; Hansen, Mark V. et al.	Chicken Soup for the Surviving Soul	Health Commun.	142,865
75	Sark	Succulent Wild Woman	Fireside	142,000
76	Tyson, Eric	Personal Finance for Dummies	IDG	142,000
77	Pearsall, Paul	The Pleasure Prescription	Hunter House	139,146
78	Daouost, Joyce & Gene	40-30-30 Fat Burning Nutrition	Wharton	138,840
79	Wells, Rebecca	Divine Secrets of the Ya-Ya Sisterhood	Haper Paperbacks	136,816
80	Eds. of Martha Stewart Living	Good Things	Clarkston Potter	135,527
81	Sunset Editors	Western Landscaping Books	Sunset	134,959
82	Moosewood Collective	Moosewood Restaurant Low Low-Fat Favorites	Clarkston Potter	134,746
83	Solomon, James	MTV's The Real World	Pocket/MTV	130,001
84	Proulx, E. Annie	Accordion Crimes	Scribner	130,000
85	Pipher, Mary	The Shelter of Each Other	Ballantine	128,448

	Author	Title	Publisher	Sold
86	Griggs, Jack	All the Birds of North America	Harper Paperbacks	127,974
87	O'Keeffe, Linda	Shoes	Workman	126,435
88	Editors of Martha Stewart Living	Christmas with Martha Stewart Living	Clarkston Potter	105,201
89	Collins, James C. & Porras, Jerry I.	Built to Last: Successful Habits of Visionary Companies	Harper Business	125,000
90	Flanagan, David	Java in a Nutshell	O'Reilly	124,268
91	Atkins, Robert C. M.D.	Dr. Atkins New Carbohydrate Gram Counter	M. Evans	124,000
92	Faulks, Sebastian	Birdsong	Vintage	123,261
93	Knapp, Caroline	Drinking: A Love Story	Dell/Delta	121,757
94	McCartney, Bill	Stand in the Gap: The Prayer Journal	Word	121,730
95	Hillman, James	The Soul's Code	Warner	121,703
96	Davis, Jim	Garfield Hams It Up (#31)	Ballantine	116,405
97	Iovine, Vicki	Girl Friend's Guide to Pregnancy	Pocket	115,542
98	Wilbur, Todd	Top Secret Restaurant Recipes	Plume	115,541
99	Shaara, Jeff	Gods and Generals	Ballantine	114,111
100	Nelson, Bob	1001 Ways to Energize Employees	Workman	113,600
101	Gray, John	Mars & Venus Together Forever	Harper Paperbacks	112,980
102	Maggio, Rosalie	How to Say It	Prentice Hall	112,600
103	Kepel, Dave & Steenland, Sally	The Magnetic Poetry Book of Poetry	Workman	112,000
104	Watterson, Bill	It's a Magical World: A Calvin & Hobbes Collection	Andrews & McMeel	110,000
105	Carlson, Richard	You Can Be Happy No Matter What	New World Library	109,000
106	Williamson, Martha	When Angels Speak	Fireside	109,000
107	Godek, Gregory J.P.	Love Coupons	Sourcebooks	103,608
108	Canfield, Jack; Hansen, Mark V. et al.	Condensed Chicken Soup for the Soul	Health Commun.	100,840
109	Lewis, Beverly	The Shunning	Bethany House	100,566

Index

About the Author

Duane S. Crowther is well-known and highly qualified as an author, publisher, editor, teacher, theologian and lecturer. He graduated with high honors from Brigham Young University with a B.A. in music education. He also holds a Masters Degree from Brigham Young University in Old and New Testament, an M.B.A. from the University of Phoenix, and has completed course work for a Ph.D. in music education at the University of Utah.

A creative and prolific author, Mr. Crowther has written more than forty books and over three dozen cassette talk tapes, plus numerous magazine articles. This extensive writing background has had a strong focus on research, and includes his writing of two master's theses and a doctoral dissertation.

Much of his writing has been in the fields of business management and the book-publishing industry. He earned his M.B.A. degree by writing monthly articles on various aspects of small business operation for various trade magazines. His contribution to the book industry includes the creation of a series of useful monographs detailing various book publishing industry practices and techniques.

He has written textbooks and complete year-long curriculum for teaching choral music in high schools and universities. Thousands of high schools have utilized his educational materials during the past two decades.

Perhaps his best-known books and tapes are on religious topics. He is widely known for his writings on the scriptures and his in-depth research in various fields including life-after-death experiences, the last days, the nature of revelation, and the spiritual gifts. His best-known books include *Prophecy—Key to the Future, The Prophecies of Joseph Smith, Gifts of the Spirit, Prophets and Prophecies of the Old Testament, Life Everlasting, Inspired Prophetic Warnings, How to Understand the Book of Mormon,* and *Teaching Choral Concepts.*

In his professional life he has served as an LDS Seminary instructor and principal, taught university classes for the BYU, University of Utah and University of Phoenix, and has taught music in the public schools. Of particular interest was his teaching of research and thesis-writing courses for the University of Phoenix. He led dozens of M.B.A. candidates to the successful completion of their theses, guiding their research on a wide variety of business projects.

Another aspect of his professional life lies in the entrepreneurial area. He has owned and managed several book and music stores. For almost three decades he has been President and the Senior Editor of Horizon Publishers & Distributors, Inc., in Bountiful, Utah, a firm which he organized in 1971.

Mr. Crowther has written and produced four patriotic pageants in the northern Utah area and has lectured at numerous business seminars, writers' seminars, BYU Education and Leadership Weeks, youth conferences and other church and community gatherings. An accomplished musician, he has taught concert band, stage band, orchestra and various choirs in the public schools. He is a talented choral director and has directed a variety of community and church choirs, including the Delta Phi returned missionaries chorus at BYU, a SPEBSQSA barbershop chorus, a community girls chorus, and large ward, stake and regional choirs. He has composed several numbers and arranged others for choral performances.

His has been a life of continued service within his church and community, and he has served in many leadership and teaching positions. The Crowthers enjoy travel and escorting travel tours. Together they have escorted several tours to Israel and various European and Middle-east countries. Mr. Crowther also has led groups to Hawaii and to Central America.

Mr. Crowther is married to the former Jean Decker, who is also an author and musician. They are the parents of eight children and reside in Bountiful, Utah.